The R__ Will Walk There

Sermons on the Life of Holiness

from the Chapel of
Nazarene Theological Seminary

Wesley D. Tracy, Editor

Beacon Hill Press of Kansas City
Kansas City, Missouri

Copyright 1983
By Beacon Hill Press of Kansas City

Printed in the United States of America

ISBN: 0-8341-0839-9

Cover Art: Crandall Vail

10   9   8   7   6   5   4   3   2   1

Permissions to quote from the following copyrighted versions of the Bible are acknowledged with appreciation:

From the *Revised Standard Version of the Bible* (RSV), copyrighted 1946, 1952, © 1971, 1973.

From the *New American Standard Bible* (NASB), © The Lockman Foundation, 1960, 1962, 1968, 1971, 1972, 1973, 1975, 1977.

From *The Holy Bible, New International Version* (NIV), copyright © 1978 by New York International Bible Society.

From the *New Testament in Modern English* (Phillips), Revised Edition © J. B. Phillips 1958, 1960, 1972. By permission of the Macmillan Publishing Co., Inc.

From the *New English Bible* (NEB), © The Delegates of the Oxford University Press and The Syndics of the Cambridge University Press, 1961, 1970.

And a highway will be there;
  it will be called the Way of Holiness.
. . . .
Only the redeemed will walk there.
                    (Isa. 35:8-9, NIV)

Contents

Editor's Preface

These sermons are not "sugar sticks." They have not been sweetened by tried-on phrases and glazed to glisten in the candy counter. Rather, they are the hearty fare of ordinary chapel addresses given by faculty members at Nazarene Theological Seminary. The sermons are more meat and potatoes than dainty petit fours.

The speakers did not prepare a sermon for publication. Instead the faculty members were simply bringing a message to aid the worship of the gathered community of scholars. The sermons, all tape-recorded as a matter of course, were collected after the fact and put together to form this volume. No particular effort was made to be sure that every aspect of the doctrine and life of holiness was covered. We simply took the sermons as they were addressed to the seminary situation. Some dimensions of this lofty theme received more emphasis than others. But we did not try to say everything. We have merely presented here a "slice of life" of the seminary experience as it relates to Christian holiness.

With the implementation of the denominational theme, "Celebrating Christian Holiness," more and more of the chapel sermons addressed this theme. I suggested to Dr. Oscar F. Reed, chairman of the Chapel Committee, and Dr. J. Kenneth Grider, chairman of the Editorial Committee, that perhaps some of the sermons could be collected and published. They thought it was a good idea, and soon the project was adopted by both committees. A subcommittee was formed made up of Oscar Reed, Kenneth Grider, and Wesley Tracy. Acting on assignment from the other members, I collected the sermons and did the basic work of preparing the manuscript for publication. Dr. Grider read all the manuscripts and assisted as liaison with the Nazarene Publishing House. Dr. Reed has written a "Homiletical Introduction" for the volume.

All the sermons in this book have been recently preached in Nazarene Theological Seminary chapel except one. Dr. Deasley's sermon was not preached in chapel, but it was offered to the seminary community, being published in the seminary paper, *The Tower.* It should also be noted that President Sander's sermon, while delivered in the seminary chapel, is a condensation of his 1982 baccalaureate address.

We offer these sermons with the prayer that their ministry may hereby be profitably extended, and that the kingdom of our Lord might in some small way be strengthened.

—WESLEY D. TRACY

A Homiletical Introduction

I often wonder what our people think when "holiness preaching" is mentioned. For some, the reply might be "Ho hum"; or "Do I have to listen to another theological lecture?", or "What is the preacher going to tell me to *do?*" Or, for others, it could be, "Here is a man who is 'bubbling over' with love, compassion, and understanding for the heart of the gospel—and I will listen with openness and responsive involvement." Holiness preaching might elicit any of these four responses.

Also, dependent on the nature of and approach to a sermon, holiness preaching can produce apathy, antagonism, or sympathetic involvement. Unfortunately, some sermons can represent sterile theological dogmatics and legalistic ethical concerns, or they can represent *a man, a message,* and *a hearer* who unite in the rediscovery of truth proclaimed with love, power, compassion, and understanding. When pastors, administrators, teachers, and evangelists are willing to do their homework, live under the burden of their task, and unite the truth of God's Word with the needs of the people, something significant happens through the preaching event in both pulpit and pew.

In this time of "authority crisis," there are two observations which may be made concerning doctrinal preaching in general and holiness preaching in particular. (1) Holiness preaching, as never before, must carry the stamp of biblical authority, finding its nexus in the Lordship of Jesus Christ. (2) Holiness preaching must demonstrate a skill in communication which will lift it out of mere theological discourse and present the truth as "story" to a congregation who must see the message within the context of its own life.

What is holiness preaching? Holiness preaching gives emphasis to the work of the Holy Spirit as the Spirit of Christ, and

9

gives regard to the whole call of God and the demand for the obedience of faith as responsive love. It includes initial sanctification, entire sanctification, growth in the Spirit, expectations under the seal of the Spirit, and guidance in the face of leadings and rebukes of the Spirit.

Holiness preaching is that scriptural proclamation that God through the death of His Son, Jesus Christ, can save and cleanse His people from all sin, fill with His love, and develop a Christlike character through the enabling power of the Holy Spirit.

In method, the proclamation of holiness should be *clear, coherent, simple,* and given with *love.* It must recognize the bipolar tension between grace and forgiveness until the hearer begins to understand that it is not what happens that is as important as his or her response to that happening; that cleansing is "love expelling evil," making the call to a holy life possible through the enabling grace of the Spirit of Christ.

A great deal of etymological exegesis and theologizing have been done on the doctrine of Christian holiness, but the field is wide open to hermeneutical approaches which, through history, tradition, structure, and language, can make the preaching dynamic and fresh in our day. We are one with Karl Barth in believing that there must be an "enthusiastic rediscovery" of truth in each generation. Otherwise, the truth is lost.

The following 12 sermons from the president and faculty of Nazarene Theological Seminary will suggest both a traditional manner of homiletical development and some novel ways which communicate the same doctrinal truth.

For one thing, the sermons are biblical; but they are developed in different homiletical forms. Secondly, not one of us is a homiletical purist; and we need not be, since we sometimes use more than one homiletical form to express our theme adequately. I sometimes tell my students that we study homiletics so that when we break the rules we will know when and why we do so.

Biblical exposition can reflect the following methods: (1) It can take a text or passage of scripture and allow the passage to speak for itself—the burdens arising directly from the Word. (2) It can take selected passages and develop burdens directly from the scriptures selected. (3) It can take a biblical passage and imply themes which are suggested but not made explicit in the passage. (4) It can also take a topic and develop the sermon thematically within the authentic suggestion of the text. These 12 sermons, for the most part, follow one of the first three, indicating the strong feeling that holiness preaching must be biblical if it is to be authentic.

Unfortunately, there is one factor missing. It is one thing to read a sermon; it is another to actually see and hear the preacher. I can assure you that these sermons were preached with a spirit which gripped the students with the truth of the message, the men modeling the kind of scriptural holiness preaching which is authentic in its insight and moving in its "drive" toward commitment.

As you read the sermons, look for the different ways the preachers approach scripture passages, and how they skillfully bring the message home to the congregation; for preaching is only preaching when substance, preacher, hearer, and ecclesiastical context come together to create a sermon-event.

—OSCAR F. REED
Professor of Preaching

1

• **Alex R. G. Deasley**

Remaining sin is the great neutralizer of the believer's vision of Christian service

Sanctification and Service

SCRIPTURE: 2 Tim. 2:15-26

TEXT: *In a great house there are not only vessels of gold and silver, but also of wood and earthenware; some to honour, and some to dishonour. If a man will cleanse himself from these, he will be a vessel unto honour: sanctified, fit for the master's use, prepared for every good work* (2 Tim. 2:20-21, author's translation).*

Throughout history the idea of service has exercised a great fascination over the minds of men. The thought of being useful speaks to something deep in the human heart. Those who labor at the highest levels of our national life think of themselves, as we also think of these, as servants or secretaries of state—or in the case of my native

---

*All Scripture quotations in this sermon are the author's own translation.

Alex R. G. Deasley
Professor of New Testament

land, as ministers of the crown. And one thought which our minds repel as intolerable is the idea that we might one day be of no use to anyone. John Milton, smitten with blindness in the middle of his career, found peace for his tormented mind only in the realization that accepting his lot with ready obedience was itself a form of divine service: "They also serve who only stand and wait." A prayer which Wesley prayed repeatedly in his last years was: "Lord, let me not live to be useless"—a prayer which God graciously answered by allowing Wesley to go on preaching to within a week of his death.

To serve God is likewise a basic instinct in the Christian soul; and our text, 2 Tim. 2:20-21, has some searching things to say about it. The passage is easily misunderstood because Paul, in very typical fashion, is not as careful as he might be to keep his metaphors straight. However, the context as a whole gives us the guidance we need. Certain preachers in the church had begun to teach that the resurrection had already taken place, meaning in effect that Christians had already received their resurrection bodies. Consequently it did not matter how they behaved with their physical bodies which they would soon be leaving: a view which was taken as a passport to licentiousness and immorality (vv. 19, 22).

Paul duly denounces them as having backslidden from the faith (v. 18) and then turns to reflecting on how such a state of affairs could arise. He gives his explanation in our text in three simple truths which lay bare the roots of effective service in the kingdom of God.

Alex R. G. Deasley, preaching from 2 Tim. 2:20-21, develops his call to "Sanctification and Service" from a textual treatment of the passage, which is the simplest form of exposition, lending itself to clarity, simplicity, and power which is so characteristic of his preaching.

1. There are two different types of Christians: the usable and the unusable (v. 20)

That is a startling statement! It is most important to grasp what Paul is *not* saying. He is not saying that in a wealthy house there are gold and silver vessels for the dining room table and rough earthenware pots for the kitchen, but every house has need of both. That is true. Paul teaches it in 1 Corinthians 12. The body needs legs and feet just as much as it needs eyes and hands. Every member has a useful role to play. But that is not what Paul is talking about here. He is talking about how a cheap earthenware vessel can—miraculously—become a silver or a golden vessel. He is talking not about usefulness but about usability. And in those terms he says that there are two different types of Christians.

That, I repeat, is a startling statement. Are not all Christians the same? "In Christ Jesus you are all sons of God through faith. . . . There is neither Jew nor Greek, slave nor free, male nor female; you are all one in Christ Jesus" (Gal. 3:28). Are not all equally loved by God, redeemed by God, sustained by God? In natural life we do not like distinctions which break us up and set us apart from each other, exalting some, debasing others. In my first day as an undergraduate at Jesus College, Cambridge, I recall well the novice's pride in being a member of Jesus College rather than any other of the 22 in the university. I also remember the shock and rebuke as the president of the college concluded his welcome address by saying loftily: "In Cambridge we do not compare one college with another. Comparisons are odious, and so are the people who make them."

It is therefore somewhat surprising and even shocking to find that the New Testament writers are making comparisons among Christians all the time. In 1 Corinthians 2—3 Paul distinguishes perfect Christians (2:6) from fleshly or carnal Christians who are embroiled in jealousy and strife, which are the negation of true spirituality (2:14—3:4). In Heb. 5:12-14 the

15

author chides those who have been Christians long enough to be able to nurture others but still require a milk diet themselves because of their spiritual immaturity which is defined as a moral thing for which they are therefore responsible (v. 14). In Phil. 1:9-10 Paul prays for his readers that their love "may abound more and more so that they may approve what is excellent and be pure and blameless for the day of Christ"; while in Eph. 3:14-21 he prays that they may be strengthened with might by God's Spirit in the inner man; that Christ may dwell in their hearts by faith; that they may come to know in understanding and experience God's love in all its dimensions, and be filled with the fullness of God.

All Christians are not the same. There are two clearly definable categories; and one category is usable by God and the other is not.

2. The difference lies in remaining sin

What is it that makes some Christians less usable than others? The answer lies in the next words: "If a man therefore cleanse himself." These simple words carry two important implications.

a. The great impediment to service is sin. "If a man will cleanse himself . . . he will be a vessel unto honour." Remaining sin in their lives is what makes Christians unusable. "Let every one who names the name of Christ depart from iniquity" (v. 19). "Shun youthful passions and follow righteousness, faith, love, peace, with them that call on the Lord out of a pure heart" (v. 22). It is sin that undermines the Christian's effectiveness. It is sin that breaks one's communion with God. It is sin that torpedoes one's power to resist temptation. Sin is the Trojan horse within the city. Sin is the fifth column within the soul which is in league with the enemy without. Sin is the traitor within the gates.

16

Have you heard of how the preaching ministry of F. B. Meyer turned on this very thing? He was already a committed Christian, but not very constant in his experience. C. T. Studd, having recently entered into the blessing himself, was touring Britain before leaving for China as a missionary and was sharing a room one night with F. B. Meyer. Meyer watched him closely and finally asked Studd: "How can I be like you?"

Studd replied: "Have you ever given yourself to Christ, for Christ to fill you?"

"I have done so in a general way," Meyer said, "but I don't know that I have done it particularly."

Studd answered: "You must do it particularly also."

That night Meyer took time to pray. "I gave God an iron ring," he said, "with all the keys of my life on it except one little key that I kept back. I said: 'Lord, I will be so devoted in everything else, but I can't live without the contents of that closet.'" Meyer was later to say: "I believe that my whole life was just hovering in the balance, and if I had kept the key of that closet, and mistrusted Christ, He never would have trusted me with the ministry of His Word." He resolved the crisis with the words: "I am not willing, but I am willing to be made willing." That was the turning point in his life. The great impediment to service is sin.

W. E. Sangster gave memorable expression to the same truth in a poem which is also a prayer.

> Lord Jesus, I am longing
>   From sin to be set free:
> To find my deep desiring
>   Forever fixed on Thee.
> All hope I now abandon
>   Myself to conquer sin;
> Invade my willing nature
>   And come and dwell within.

The passing years oppress me,
My growth in grace so slow:
My wayward, fickle cravings
Have leagued me to the foe;
Myself to self disloyal,
I loathe yet love my sin:
Now hear my heartfelt pleading
And come and dwell within.

If Thou should'st stand close by me,
'Tis more than I deserve;
But, being still outside me,
From virtue yet I swerve.
Come nearer, Lord, than near me,
My succour to begin;
Usurp the heart that craves Thee!
Oh, come and dwell within.

Remaining sin is the great enemy. But the text tells us more than this. The words, "If a man will cleanse himself . . . he will be a vessel unto honour" imply something else: namely that

b. *Remaining sin can be cleansed.* The word "cleanse" is not a characteristically Pauline word: it is typical rather of John and Hebrews. The remarkable thing is that, on the few occasions Paul uses it, he uses it of the cleansing of sin from the lives of Christians. (That is not always so elsewhere in the New Testament, especially in Hebrews where it has a specialized sense; and we must be careful not to make it carry more exegetical freight than it can bear.) "Having therefore these promises, dearly beloved, let us cleanse ourselves from all impurity of the flesh and spirit, perfecting holiness in the fear of God" (2 Cor. 7:1). "He gave himself for us that he might redeem us from all iniquity and cleanse for himself a people of his own, zealous of good works" (Titus 2:14). This is especially true with the intensive form of the word used here which is found elsewhere only in 1 Cor. 5:7:

"Cleanse out the old leaven that you may be a new lump."
Remaining sin can be cleansed!

That is marvelous good news! It is good news of a miracle!
So many of our important capacities in life are fixed: our looks,
our brains, our constitution. But in the life of the spirit, miracles
are possible, and unusable Christians can be made usable. This is
where Paul's metaphor breaks down. In the natural order it is
impossible for an earthen pot to be changed into a golden or
silver pot; but what is impossible naturally is possible spiritually.
And while it would be exegetical license to say that Paul's words
were intended to convey that point, that is the point which—in
spite of themselves—they convey. The greatest democracy on
earth is the democracy of faith. Promotion in God's service
depends not on pedigree or length of service, but on cleansing,
and that is equally available to all: "If a man will cleanse himself."

Not that we can cleanse *ourselves*. But when the New Testament writers think of our responsibility to cooperate with the
grace that God provides, they often speak in this way. "Every
man who has this hope in him purifies himself" (1 John 3:3).
And if we cleanse ourselves, we can become "vessels unto honour."

3. The key to service is sanctification

"If a man will cleanse himself . . . he will be a vessel unto
honour: sanctified, fit for the master's use, prepared for every
good work" (v. 21).

There are three marks of the usable Christian.

a. Sanctification. You will note that the translations differ
at this point. RSV has "consecrated," NEB has "dedicated," NIV
has "made holy," KJV has "sanctified." You are well aware that
the Greek word "sanctify" *(hagiazō)* which is used here has as its
root meaning "to set apart," that is, for God's service. However,
it is a familiar feature in the New Testament for those who are
sanctified in the sense of being set apart to be exhorted to be

19

fully sanctified in a moral sense. In a way, that is inevitable in a truly moral religion, for the only thing that is fit for God's service is that which has been not merely dedicated, but that which has been cleansed. There is a point at which the distinction vanishes. The meaning in our present text is clear. Sanctification is linked directly with cleansing: "If a man will *cleanse* himself . . . he will be . . . sanctified." "Sanctified" in the moral sense is the only possible meaning here.

The point of particular significance is that sanctification is named first in the qualities of the usable Christian. The whole chain of preparation has been finely summed up in the dictum of J. Sidlow Baxter:

> *What I give He takes;*
> *What He takes He cleanses;*
> *What He cleanses He fills;*
> *What He fills He uses.*

b. The second mark of the usable Christian, after sanctification, is *serviceability:* "Fit for the master's use." It is only when we are sanctified that we are fully serviceable. The underlying picture is that of a wealthy house in which only the best tableware is fit for the use of the master. In Britain there is an institution or custom known as royal patents. On all sorts of products from steak sauce up you will see the royal coat of arms and under it the formula: "By appointment: makers of steak sauce to Her Majesty Queen Elizabeth II." These patents are issued at the beginning of each reign; and there is fierce competition among manufacturers to gain a coveted royal patent, for this advertises to the world that their produce is fit for the Queen's table.

Paul is saying, in effect, that there is another royal patent; that our lives may be so changed as to meet God's approval; and that when we are sanctified, we receive the stamp of serviceability: "By appointment: fit for the Master's use."

c. The third mark of the usable Christian is *versatility:* "Prepared for every good work." There are indeed gifts which equip specific individuals for specific tasks. But there is also a Spirit-filled versatility in the New Testament; and it is striking how frequently it is associated with the language of perfection. "Now the God of peace . . . make you perfect in every good work to do his will" (Heb. 13:21). "All scripture is given by inspiration of God . . . that the man of God may be perfect, thoroughly furnished unto every good work" (2 Tim. 3:17). "He gave himself for us that he might redeem us from all iniquity and purify for himself a people of his own possession, zealous of good works" (Titus 2:14). It does not matter how many gifts we have: there are some good works we shall never do and can never do until we are "sanctified, fit for the master's use, prepared for every good work." Sanctification is the fundamental qualification and the comprehensive qualification.

The Christian Church in our times is greatly exercised about service, and we are exhorted on all hands—and rightly—to get involved. Peter Taylor Forsyth once said in his penetrating way: "The greatest service I owe the kingdom of God is my personal holiness." Paul is saying the same thing: The best preparation for service is sanctification. "In a great house there are not only vessels of gold and silver, but also of wood and earthenware; some to honour, and some to dishonour. If a man will cleanse himself from these, he will be a vessel unto honour: sanctified, fit for the master's use, prepared for every good work."

2

• **J. Kenneth Grider**

*Entire sanctification
comes after regeneration
and is instantaneously received*

God's Will:
Our Entire Sanctification

TEXT: *For this is the will of God, your sanctification* (1 Thess.
4:3, NASB).*

You have probably already received entire sanctification. In that case, reflect on this work of grace with me, and celebrate God's provision made possible through Jesus Christ's incarnation, death, and resurrection. If entire sanctification has not become an event for you, hear the word as to what can occur.

The subject of this message is "God's Will: Our Entire Sanctification." The text is 1 Thess. 4:3: "For this is the will of God, your sanctification."

---

*Unless otherwise stated, all Scripture quotations in this sermon are from the *New American Standard Bible.*

J. Kenneth Grider
Professor of Theology

1. Consider the text with me first from this standpoint: *that this sanctification would be subsequent to their regeneration*

It would be because, according to Acts 17, when Paul had preached Christ three sabbath days in Thessalonica, some Jews "were persuaded" and "a great multitude of the God-fearing Greeks and a number of the leading women" (Acts 17:4).

Paul, then, is writing to a church full of believers who had accepted Christ when he had preached there.

This sanctification would also be subsequent to their regeneration because of the way Paul refers to the Thessalonians all through this Epistle—as "brothers." Actually, he calls them brothers 14 times in this five-chapter letter—meaning by that, no doubt, both brothers and sisters. And "brothers," or "brethren," is one of the New Testament's words for "Christians."

This sanctification, further, would have been subsequent to their regeneration because Paul refers to them as "you believers" (2:10), and as "you who believe" (2:13). "Believers" is one of the New Testament's names for converted persons. They are "disciples" sometimes, they are persons of the "church" often, they are the people of the "way," et cetera, and they are "believers."

Further still, this sanctification would be subsequent to their regeneration because of what Paul says about them in chapter 1. He says, "You also became imitators of us and of the Lord, having received the word" (v. 6). Besides having "received the word," they had become examples in witnessing for Christ.

J. Kenneth Grider, senior faculty member, develops a theological affirmation with strong scriptural support from First Thessalonians, using the contextual and etymological materials to argue the case for secondness, immediacy, and cleansing. The sermon is instructional and lends itself to an environment in which a congregation is seeking enlightenment.

Paul says, "You became an example to all the believers . . . for the word of the Lord has sounded forth from you" (vv. 7-8). Paul exaggerates, in commending them on their witnessing, saying they had witnessed so well that he did not need to witness. He says, "The word of the Lord has sounded forth from you, not only in Macedonia [where Thessalonica was located] and Achaia [where Paul was then, in Corinth], but also in every place your faith toward God has gone forth, so that we have no need to say anything" (v. 8).

Further yet, this sanctification would be subsequent to their regeneration because they are already said to be people of faith. Paul says, "Timothy has come to us from you, and has brought us good news of your faith" (3:6). And he adds, "For this reason, brethren, in all our distress and affliction we were comforted about you through your faith" (3:7).

The past two Sundays, at Sunday School, we have been discussing Israel's deliverance from Egypt and her entering into Canaan. In holiness circles, Israel's deliverance from Egypt's bondage has long been understood properly as typifying our justification. Her encampment in Canaan typifies our entire sanctification. The Thessalonians had been delivered from bondage to acts of sin, and Paul is telling them that God's will is their Canaan privilege of entire sanctification.

2. But this sanctification as God's will for the Thessalonians would not only have been subsequent to their regeneration; *it would have been received instantaneously*

Our text, "This is the will of God, your sanctification," has in it "sanctification," a noun—not a verb. Thus no tense is in this word itself, by which we see how this sanctification would be implemented. Yet at a number of other places in this letter, where Paul presses them about their urgent need, verbs *are*

24

used, and they are in the aorist tense, which denotes decisive, instantaneous, or completed action.

In 3:10, the NASB's "complete" is aorist, which Daniel Steele, Boston University's exegete, was fond of calling the "lightning tense." In 3:10 we read, "We night and day keep praying most earnestly that we may see your face, and may complete what is lacking in your faith." This something that was lacking "in their faith," as brothers, as believers, as witnesses, was the "sanctification" which was God's will for them. Paul is earnestly praying that he might "complete" (NASB), "perfect" (KJV), "supply" (RSV, NIV) their lack, namely, "sanctification." And this word, rendered in these various ways, is aorist in tense, denoting that Paul was not praying for a gradual sanctification, but for one that would be punctiliar, crisic, momentary. If his prayer had been for a gradual completion, this word would have been in the present tense. A. T. Robertson, the outstanding Calvinist exegete, says, "The three kinds of action [aorist, present, perfect] are thus momentary or punctiliar when action is regarded as a whole and may be represented by a dot (.); linear or durative action which may be represented by a continuous line (——); the continuance of perfected or completed action which may be represented by this graph (.——)" (*A Grammar of the New Testament in the Light of Historical Research* [New York: Doran, 1949], p. 825).

I feel I need to take a bit of time to discuss this aorist tense because its significance as implying the immediacy of a sanctification that is entire is sometimes questioned. And I would admit that such figures as circumcision (Col. 2:10-11) and sealing (Eph. 1:13; 2 Cor. 1:22) imply the immediacy of entire sanctification more indisputably. Yet I agree with H. Orton Wiley that the aorist tense "denotes a momentary, completed act without reference to time" (*Christian Theology,* NPH, 2:447). I agree with W. T. Purkiser, who calls the use of this tense an "impressive line of evidence for the instantaneousness of sanctification"

(*Conflicting Concepts of Holiness*, NPH, p. 34). I also agree with longtime Greek professor Richard Howard, who says that "the basic significance of the aorist . . . is that it depicts a *crisis act* in distinction from a progressive process" (*Newness of Life*, NPH, p. 170). I know that in John 2:20 the aorist is used for "build," in reference to the Temple, which took 46 years to build; and such uses are why I am saying that completed action is also denoted by the aorist tense. If God's will is for a completed sanctification, we are still not talking about a gradual one that never becomes completed during this life. Also, the older holiness writers, such as S. S. White, my predecessor in theology here, I feel, had a point in saying that since entire sanctification is God's work, and not ours, it is instantaneously wrought. The building of the Temple was a work of people, and it took 46 years. Consecration, which is one aspect of our part in entire sanctification, is gradual; but when, after our consecration is complete, and after God helps us to exercise faith, God sanctifies us wholly in an instantaneous act. As Wiley says, there is a "cleansing at a single stroke of inbred sin" (*Christian Theology,* 2:446).

Having said something about the aorist tense itself, let us further note its use in this area of First Thessalonians. Besides its being the tense of "supply" in 3:10, it is the tense of "increase" and "abound" in 3:12, where Paul says, "May the Lord cause you to increase and abound in love for one another, and for all men." Those words sound gradual to us, in the English. But since they are in the aorist tense, they are in keeping with the "supply" of 3:10. Paul hopes for a special step-up in their love for each other, and for "all men," perhaps including their enemies who had run Paul and his party out of town.

This connects with the fact that, in Matt. 5:48, the exhortation to "be perfect, as your heavenly Father is perfect" is in the context of the exhortation to "love your enemies" (v. 44). When "the love of God has been poured out within our hearts through the Holy Spirit who was given to us," as Paul says to the

Romans in 5:5, a special quality of love is possible, which John calls "perfect love" (1 John 4:8)—because it is not now mixed with the carnal "give me" and "me first" motivations.

Still meaning to treat the instantaneousness of this sanctification which is God's will, from the standpoint of the aorist tense which Paul uses, let me mention that "establish" is also aorist in 3:13 where Paul says, "So that He may establish your hearts unblamable in holiness before our God and Father." Again it would not be a gradual establishment, but one that God would bring about instantaneously by sanctifying them.

It would make them "unblamable." Faultlessness awaits the next life, for Jude says that God will later "present" us "before his glorious presence without fault" (NIV), "faultless" (KJV). The NASB uses "blameless" in Jude 24, and therefore neglects to reveal the difference between "blameless" and "faultless," which Arndt and Gingrich supports, and which holiness writers have properly taught for generations.

Still another instance of the aorist tense, as indicating the instantaneousness of the sanctification that is God's will for these believers, is in the word for "sanctify" in 5:23. In what might be called the summit passage of this Epistle, Paul writes, "May the God of peace Himself sanctify you entirely" (5:23).

Note that it is God, God the Father, who sanctifies us—"the God of peace Himself." Even as God justifies us, He sanctifies us. And even as we repent in preparation for justification, we consecrate in preparation for entire sanctification. Dr. Ralph Earle, Dr. Roy Swim, and Dr. J. A. Huffman convinced the RSV translating committee that the Greek makes this kind of distinction between "consecration" and "sanctification," and secured all 18 changes they asked for in the original publication (1952). "Consecrate" was changed to "sanctify."

Note also that the subjunctive-mood "prayer" is that God would sanctify them "entirely"—"wholly" (KJV); "through and through" (NIV). Even as depravity is total, extending to all the

27

aspects of our nature, so is the sanctification in which God cleanses it away.

The word, here, is *holoteleis*, a compound of the words for "whole," and "complete" or "entire." This strong, compound word is used by Paul, here, of the sanctification which is God's will for the Thessalonians (in 4:3) and which he here prays will happen. The prayer is that, even as their Adamic depravity was total (see Rom. 5:12-21; 7:14-25), the cleansing from it would be total also (see Matt. 3:11-12; Acts 15:8-9). The compound word "wholly-completely" is even further supported by Paul's next words, in which he lists what was commonly thought of in the Greek world as the three aspects of human nature (body, soul, and spirit) as areas of their natures that would be cleansed by this sanctification. He says, "May your spirit and soul and body be preserved complete, without blame" (5:23). (Even the "preserved," here, is aorist in tense.)

Most versions translate the next words as "at the coming of our Lord Jesus Christ," as though they are to be preserved at that time. And "at" is a quite usual translation of the small Greek word here. Yet I view this passage as meaning what is in the Phillips translation, where we read, "until the coming of our Lord Jesus Christ." As I grew up on a farm, we preserved food "until" a later time. And I do not know why Paul would be concerned about their entire sanctification, and about their being "kept" (Phillips) or "preserved," *at* Christ's coming. On that basis, he would have been urging their glorification. Yet the New Testament does not urge glorification. What will happen then will happen sovereignly—by God's own sovereign action—and is neither prayed for nor urged upon people.

This glorification at the time of the Second Coming would not be something lacking in their faith. It is not what was concerning the apostle at that time. What *was* concerning him was that these believers might receive a through-and-through cleansing which would steady and sturdy them, establish them in the best of times and in the worst of times, until the *parousia*, after which the kingdoms of this world will become the kingdoms of God's dear Son.

I have meant to show two things, mainly, from this Epistle, and particularly from our text, "This is the will of God, your sanctification." I have meant to show that this sanctification that was God's will *would be subsequent to their regeneration.* I have also meant to show that it *would be received instantaneously.*

In closing, let me say that this entire sanctification, subsequent to our regeneration and received instantaneously, as a through and through cleansing, is in some ways analogous to vinyl, the floor covering so often used these days.

Some of you have lived in houses where your linoleum only had an imprint on its surface, and the imprint or design soon wore off. How many of you have had linoleum of that type? Nod, or raise your hand, and admit it. Right. Many of us have had. As I grew up, at our cook stove in the kitchen, and at our water bucket, the imprint soon got worn off.

In vinyl, the design, the imprint, runs throughout the material. Walk on it, scuff it, scrape it, mistreat it, and the design is still there. It is that way with entire, through-and-through sanctification. When God in His graciousness cleanses us in this way, the imprint of the divine, in the economy of the Father's grace, runs throughout these natures of ours: body, soul, spirit, mind, heart, and whatever else there is in the stuff of you and me. This kind of cleansing was God's will for the Thessalonian believers. It is the kind of cleansing already implemented in the lives of most of us here this morning. And it will be God's will for many believing and loving and hoping Christians to whom you designated young learners will be ministering in the next several decades in these grand and awful times.

3

● **Charles Shaver**

After Calvary God has a right to be trusted

Set Free by the Spirit

TEXT: *Therefore, there is now no condemnation for those who are in Christ Jesus, because through Christ Jesus the law of the Spirit of life set me free from the law of sin and death. For what the law was powerless to do in that it was weakened by the sinful nature, God did by sending his own Son in the likeness of sinful man to be a sin offering. And so he condemned sin in sinful man, in order that the righteous requirements of the law might be fully met in us, who do not live according to the sinful nature but according to the Spirit* (Rom. 8:1-4, NIV).*

Visit an automobile showroom with me. Imagine that my family is about to purchase a new car. My daughters, Rachel and Miriam, have pronounced their joint appraisal, "Dad, it's beautiful." My son, Paul, has had

---

*Unless otherwise indicated, all Scripture quotations in this chapter are from the *New International Version.*

Charles Shaver
Professor of Evangelism

30

his head stuck under the hood and decides it's got plenty of power. We tell the salesman we'll take it. The children jump in the backseat, and I help my wife, Nancy, in on the passenger side of the front seat. I take one final look at four happy faces inside the car and ask, "All set?" "All set!" they chorus back. Imagine then that I would step around to the rear of the car, firmly plant my hands against the rear bumper, and laboriously push it out of the automobile showroom and all the way home. How ridiculous to buy all that power under the hood and then push the car home!

And yet how many Christians there are who have all kinds of potential for spiritual power and are trying to live their Christian lives in their own strength instead of drawing on the greatest source of power the New Testament has revealed—the power of the Holy Spirit. In this eighth chapter of Romans the Holy Spirit is mentioned no fewer than 19 times. We have the tremendous promise of power in Rom. 8:2: "Through Christ Jesus the law of the Spirit of life set me free from the law of sin and death." So I invite you to draw on the resources of New Testament power, the power of the Spirit.

1. Verse 1 tells us, "Therefore, there is now no condemnation"

The word "therefore" is like a hinge, and the hinge that opens into the truth of the eighth chapter is securely fastened to the difficulties of the seventh chapter. In chapter 7, what Paul has told is almost like a mathematical equation: The law of God plus the law of the mind has resulted in the law of sin. According to Rom. 7:23, this law of sin means that man has been made a

---

"Set Free by the Spirit," by Charles "Chic" Shaver, is evangelistic in motive, with interesting and challenging illustrative materials. The structure of the message is expositional, the burdens taken directly from the text. Who said that evangelistic sermons must always be thematic?

prisoner. In that condition, Paul looks around for rescue. The rescue is spoken of in verses 24 and 25 of that seventh chapter, "What a wretched man I am! Who will rescue me from this body of death? Thanks be to God—through Jesus Christ our Lord!" When Jesus Christ puts in His appearance, it makes a difference. So the eighth chapter begins with a "therefore." A new door has opened. A new time has come. Jesus Christ is on the scene. "Therefore, there is now no condemnation."

The eighth chapter is filled with contrasts. Whereas before, mankind was locked into a particular pattern of living, now that Jesus Christ is come a new possibility rises before us. In Rom. 8:1-4, instead of the law of sin, we may now have the law of the Spirit. In verses 5-8, instead of the carnal mind, we may now have the spiritual mind. In verses 9-11, instead of death we may now have life. In verses 12-13, instead of obligation to the sinful nature, we now have obligation to the Holy Spirit. A new day has dawned. There is no condemnation.

Did you know that God wants you to live without condemnation? Some people act as if God wants them to go around all the time with a dark cloud over their heads. Some people act as if God is just waiting to catch them so He can pour guilt on them. But the New Testament teaches that it is our privilege that there be "now no condemnation." Some people hover under condemnation because they have a misunderstanding of what sin is. Their concept of sin is too severe. Even the New Testament makes distinction between known sin and that which is not known. Remember James declared, "Anyone, then, who knows the good he ought to do and doesn't do it, sins" (4:17). This implies that the man has to *know* of the opportunity; the failure to take the opportunity is sin. If he does not *know*, it is not regarded in the same way as if he *does* know. Some people have condemnation because they misunderstand this.

Some have condemnation because they have a low view of themselves. The Scripture seems to imply that there is a natural, normal, God-given appreciation of self, so loving your neighbor is patterned on loving yourself.

But though some condemnation comes from a wrong concept of sin, and some condemnation comes from low self-esteem, most condemnation comes because people disobey God. That problem you may be freed from because of Christ. We are not under the law (Rom. 6:14). We are not in the flesh (8:9). We are in Jesus Christ, and in Christ there is now no condemnation.

2. Verse 2 speaks of another kind of freedom: "Because through Christ Jesus the law of the Spirit of life set me free from the law of sin and death"

There are two laws in this verse. The law of sin and death is not like the law that is passed by the city council in which on a 5-4 vote they increase the fine for going through stop signs. The law in verse 2 is a regulative principle of life. It is something built into the fabric of things. It is like the law of gravity which is a part of the way our world operates. The law of gravity is not passed by a city council. The law of gravity is built into the fabric of our world, and in the falling of man away from God, a law was written on the hearts of mankind. In Rom. 7:22-23, Paul identifies this law: "In my inner being I delight in God's law; but I see *another law* at work in the members of my body, waging war against the *law of my mind* and making me a prisoner of the *law of sin* at work within my members" (emphasis added).

It is this regulative principle that produces sins. Just as the law of gravity will drag a person down to the ground, so the law of sin and death is constantly working within a person to drag him or her down to sin. It is called the law of sin and death because sin always produces death.

But I'm glad to tell you that there is another law. It is "the law of the Spirit of life in Christ Jesus" (8:2, KJV). This is also a regulative principle. This is something written into the fabric of things, written into the fabric of spiritual life. It is an inward

33

force impelling to action. It is a law of the Spirit, because this law of life is created by the Holy Spirit. Long before the New Testament came along, Ezekiel prophesied in 36:27, "I will put my Spirit in you and move you to . . . keep my laws." Paul was later to write "God . . . worketh in you, both to will and to do of his good pleasure" (Phil. 2:13, KJV). It is a law of the Spirit written on our hearts, changing us from within.

What if I were giving you this message on Sunday morning and addressed you right up to noontime and then gave you a command? Most people don't like to be told what to do. But let's assume that at 12 noon I gave you this command: "Go to lunch now." That would not be such a hard command to obey. Though that is an external command, there is something about your inward makeup, something called the law of hunger that is written all over your stomach so that when a fellow would say to you, "Go to lunch now," something inside of you would say, "That's a good idea. I think I will." When there's an inward disposition to receive the command, it is easy to obey. God wants to send His Spirit into your heart and write His law there. Then you will want to do what He wants you to do. You will be able to sing with the Psalmist, "I delight to do thy will, O my God: yea, thy law is within my heart" (Ps. 40:8, KJV).

The law of the Spirit will set us free from the law of sin and death. The word here for "set free" is the same word used in Rom. 6:18 and 22, where it means "set free from sin." The verb form indicates that the setting free is something which God does suddenly in a moment of time, not a long, drawn-out process. God wants to set you and me free from the law of sin and death. I hope you will make it as personal as Paul made it. Then you will be able to testify, "Through Christ Jesus, the law of the Spirit of life has set me free."

"Through Christ Jesus the law of the Spirit of life set me free from the law of sin and death." Recently we had the worst winter in Kansas City that I can remember. I said to myself, "It would sure be nice if I could go visit my mom. I haven't seen her for a long time." My mother lives in Florida. I looked at my schedule and I could find only three days of free time to go to Florida. Ever since I've been a little kid, I've had this problem— no matter how fast I've tried to walk or I've tried to run, I have never been able to cover the territory from Kansas City to Florida and back again in three days. Ever since I've been a little kid, there's been this law of gravity that seems to make my steps very short, my stride very limited, the distance covered slight. Lately I've been jogging and I've finally gotten to the place where I've achieved a four-minute half mile, but even with that, I couldn't make it from Kansas City to Florida and back in three days. Then one of my friends came around and said: "You shouldn't let that keep you from going—just because you can't run very fast, just because the law of gravity is always holding you down. Haven't you heard? There's another law you need to know about. It's called the law of aerodynamics. You see, they have these jet planes that you can go on. Those jet planes have the ability to go much faster than people."

"I don't understand jet planes," I said.

He said, "That doesn't matter. You don't have to understand jet planes. Jet planes have enough power to do it."

"What does it take?" I said.

He said, "You've got to get on one and ride it."

So I got my courage up and went to the airport, and I got on a jet plane. I didn't know how it would run, but I just had to have full confidence in the plane and the persons flying it. I rested back in the seat and I put my full weight upon the resources of that aircraft. The plane taxied down to the end of the runway. Up to now it was still on the ground. The law of gravity was still in effect. Then the plane began to pick up speed and finally it got to a point where the law of aerodynamics took over. All of a sudden the plane left the ground, and in three hours I was in Florida. The law of aerodynamics had set me free from the law of gravity.

But I want to tell you there was a day in my spiritual life that was even more phenomenal. For nearly one year after my conversion to Christ, I had been struggling and battling with an inner selfishness in my heart that I couldn't seem to control. I didn't want it there, but I didn't seem to be able to cast it out in my strength. On September 2, 1956, at 9:30 in the evening, the Holy Spirit came in fullness to my heart, and He set me free from the law of sin and death. My Christian life took on a permanently higher level. It can happen to you too.

3. **The third verse tells us what God did by sending His Son: "For what the law was powerless to do in that it was weakened by the sinful nature, God did by sending his own Son in the likeness of sinful man to be a sin offering"**

Now the law told us what to do, but the law did not have power to equip us to do what it told us to do. It just told us. And since to begin with I had only a sinful nature to respond to what God told me to do, there was resistance and rebellion. God sent His Son who became a sin offering for me. The law told us what to do, we couldn't do it, and so God did.

You say, "I'm afraid to come to God. He knows all about me." You say, "I'm afraid to come to God. God is all-powerful. He could crush me." You say, "I'm afraid to come to God. God is holy and I am unholy." But I want to tell you that besides all that, God is love, God loves you, and if He loves you, you don't have to be afraid to come to Him.

By sending Christ to the earth, and Christ going to the Cross, God condemned sin. The word here does not mean condemn in the sense of merely expressing disapproval. The law had already condemned sin. It means God pronounced the doom of sin. God condemned and pronounced the doom of sin in the flesh by the coming of Jesus Christ, and because He is God and has condemned sin in the flesh, we need not be condemned anymore.

4. The fourth verse tells us of the importance of living by the Spirit: "In order that the righteous requirements of the law might be fully met in us, who do not live according to the sinful nature but according to the Spirit"

The things that have been happening in verses 1-3: the concern of God, the coming of Jesus Christ, the giving of the Spirit, are *in order that* the righteous requirements of the law might be met in us. Finally man has arrived at God's goal. Do you notice how personal it has been? In verse 1 there is no condemnation for *those* who are in Christ Jesus. In verse 2 the law of the Spirit of life has set *me* free. And in verse 4, the righteous requirements of the law can be fully met *in us*. In "those," in "me," in "us." Not in haloed saints, not in spiritual specialists, not in heavenly angels, but in us—"the righteous requirements of the law might be fully met in us."

We are taught in Rom. 8:2 that by the grace of God it is possible to be delivered from the principle of sin. But we must be realistic and realize that whereas in a moment of time God's Spirit can free us from the law of sin, the Scripture also teaches us that we still live in physically limited bodies. Our bodies are under the effects of sin. We do not have perfect mental judgment. Our verbal expression is not always what it ought to be. Verse 23 recognizes this, and says, "Not only so, but we ourselves, who have the firstfruits of the Spirit, groan inwardly as we wait eagerly for our adoption as sons." If you read this in context, you find that the Holy Spirit is God's initial Pledge, God's Firstfruit, His seal and approval upon us, until we come to the place where our bodies are redeemed in the coming of Jesus Christ and the resurrection of the body. So God can cleanse your heart from all sin, but you will still be living in a limited body.

Now there's another insight in 8:26: "In this same way, the Spirit helps us in our weakness. We do not know what we ought to pray, but the Spirit himself intercedes for us." You see, we don't know what we ought to pray for. The Spirit *frees* us from the law of sin and death, but the Spirit only *helps* our weaknesses. We are *cleansed* from *sin* by the Spirit, but we are only *helped* by the Spirit in our human limitations. Keep the teaching about the Spirit balanced. Don't make it to be more than the Bible makes it, but make it all the Bible makes it.

The Bible says that if this righteous requirement is going to be fulfilled in us, we must live not according to the sinful nature but according to the Spirit. The King James says, "That the righteousness of the law might be fulfilled in us, who walk not after the flesh, but after the Spirit." To walk means you take a step at a time. There is a moment in time when the Spirit frees us suddenly from the law of sin and death. But there is also a moment-by-moment walk in the Spirit after we have been filled with the Spirit.

Let's go back to the airplane again. I'm flying now from Kansas City to Florida, and I have found the plane has sufficient power to overcome the law of gravity and the law of aerodynamics has lifted me off the ground. I'm on my way, two hours into the flight. I begin to get a little concerned. I look around me and say, "Well, I'm not sure I like all these passengers on the plane. I'm not sure that this pilot is doing such a good job after all. I'm pretty sufficient in myself, and I think if I were given another chance, I could probably make it on my own. I don't think this plane's so great. I mean, it got me off the ground, but who says I can't make it the rest of the way on my own."

I look to the right of me and there is a little red handle under that window. It says, "Emergency Exit." So I just turn that handle, and I open the window. I step out into the air on my own, flying over Georgia, 25,000 feet high, and I say that I'm going on my way to Florida by myself. If I take the control back into my own hands and my own powers, the law of gravity takes over again. I would plummet to my death.

Many people have started out in the Spirit-filled life and can point to a definite time when they have been filled with the Spirit, but they have not yet learned the secret of walking in the Spirit on a moment-by-moment basis. We must be filled with the Spirit, but also must walk in the Spirit moment by moment. We enter by faith and continue by faith. Don't try to take the power back into your own hands.

You may ask, "How do I enter into this victorious Christian life? I know Christ is my Savior, I know I've begun to follow the Lord, but I have this same inner battle with selfishness that you talk about. There are some places where my following the Lord is sorely tested, and I find selfishness rising up. There are attitudes I can't control. I cannot say I'm 100 percent God's. I feel I'm mostly God's, but not 100 percent. How would I enter this life of victory?"

The answer in two words is: *surrender* and *faith.* A surrender to God without reservation. And faith to believe God to do what He came to do, to believe the Spirit to fill, to believe the Spirit to cleanse, to believe that the law of the Spirit of life in Christ Jesus will set you free from the law of sin and death. You may be afraid. It seems that Paul anticipated your fear. Look at Rom. 8:32. If He has already given us His only Son, Jesus Christ, will He not give you anything and everything else you need to successfully complete the journey?

It was a good day for me when all of my children had entered their teenage years. When they became teenagers, I noticed that their attitudes changed, and though all their maturing had not happened yet, it was sure a big improvement over the fourth grade. I've thought back to when Paul was 13 and Miriam had just turned 12. They had now been out to a few other homes, and they decided that our home was really a lot better than they originally thought it was. They felt like there was more love in our home than they had realized. And if you'll imagine now with me a bit, let's let Paul be the spokesman. "Well, Dad, I'm 13 now, and I've been looking around at things.

39

Now that I'm big, I've got a better view of life. I've decided after being at this buddy's house and being at that buddy's house and going to school and talking to the other kids, and looking around the scene—I've come to the conclusion, Dad, that you're not so bad after all. I'm beginning to realize that maybe the thing you want more than anything else is for everything to turn out just right for Miriam and me.

"And so, Dad, Miriam and I have talked it over. We know there have been times when we have not always obeyed you. There have been times when we've done the right thing because we thought we'd get in trouble if we didn't, but on the inside we never wanted to do it in the first place. But, Dad, now that we've thought it through, we've decided that you really do love us and that you want only the best for us. We have decided we are going to give ourselves to you without a reservation. We will do what you tell us to do, we will accept your wisdom, we will take you at your word. Dad, we are unreservedly yours."

What do you think I would say if he said that to me? Do you think I would say, "Oh, good, now I've got you, and now that you've agreed to do that, I am going to hide your roller skates. I'm going to burn up your baseball glove, I'm going to pour Drano in your fish tank. I'm going to drown your parakeet in the bathtub. There'll be no Saturday morning cartoons. And you will eat asparagus for breakfast every day of your life. Now I've got you!"

Can you, in your wildest imagination, think I would say that? Of course not! And if I, as a father, wouldn't say that to my son, why would you be afraid to give yourself completely to God the Father? "If ye then, being evil, know how to give good gifts unto your children: how much more shall your heavenly Father give the Holy Spirit to them that ask him?" (Luke 11:13, KJV). Would you surrender all and trust Him to set you free from all sin by the Spirit's power?

4

● **Wesley D. Tracy**

*The three rings of truth which give integrity
to the holy life form a matched, interlocking
set. To separate them is wrong, even disgraceful*

Rings of Truth

SCRIPTURE: 1 John 1:5—2:6

TEXT: *If we walk in the light, as he is in the light, we have
fellowship with one another, and the blood of Jesus his
Son cleanses us from all sin* (1 John 1:7, RSV).

A ring forms a circle. Being
a circle, it has no end; and having no end, a ring can symbolize
eternity. Some wedding ceremonies celebrate the ring as a precious symbol of eternal love. This comparison is not an inappropriate way to symbolize the truths of 1 John which many
Christians treasure.

The ring symbol well fits John's method of presenting divine truth. John does not present his information in syllogistic,
linear thought like we do. Rather, his presentation is cyclical,
circular if you please. That is not to say that the apostle wrote in

Wesley D. Tracy
Associate Professor of Religious Education

circles, but it is to say that John presents "rings of truth" to us. He touches on a divine truth, then, cyclically he comes back to it again and again. Thus the Epistle is a series of interlocking rings of truth as beautiful as Hawaiian leis, as precious as rings of gold, as eternal as Calvary love.

I want to invite you to explore with me three rings of truth from the passage we have just read.

1. The first "ring of truth" is that God has done something miraculous *for* us

Let's look at this ring of truth.

"The Father sent the Son to be the Saviour of the world" (4:14).

"He is the atoning sacrifice for our sins, and not only for ours but also for the sins of the whole world" (2:2, NIV).

And completing the ring:

"He sent his one and only Son into the world . . . He loved us and sent his Son as an atoning sacrifice for our sins" (4:9-10, NIV).

The band of golden truth here formed has profound meanings. But whatever else it may signify, it proclaims the miracle of grace called justification. Christ is the Expiation, the Propitiation, the atoning Sacrifice for my sins and yours. What God has done *for* me is to justify me freely.

Paul celebrates this truth also. He declares that we are "justified freely by his grace." Christ was "set forth to be a propitiation through faith in his blood" (Rom. 3:24-25). Paul

---

Wesley Tracy has taken an intriguing theme and skillfully applied it inferentially from 1 John 1:5—2:6. The confessional nature of his sermon unites the proclamation with the hearers in a sermon-event which is the objective of every preacher. Notice the way that he uses various collateral scriptures to support his theme.

says again, "While we were yet sinners, Christ died for us" (5:8); and "therefore being justified by faith, we have peace with God" (v. 1); for as he asserts in Col. 1:20, Christ "made peace through the blood of his cross."

God has done something miraculous for us. Through Christ's atonement He justifies us freely, disregarding all the sins of all the past.

Do we need this miracle of grace? Picture yourself in the eternal Court of Justice—justice with a capital *J.* There you stand as guilty as sin. You are clothed in the stained shirt of sin and in the ragged breeches of mildewed self-righteousness. In His presence you suddenly recognize the ridiculous inappropriateness of your attire. What will you as a condemned and hopeless sinner do? Oh, you are resourceful so you will try something. The sequence usually follows this order:

a. Blame someone else—your parents, pastor, or society. But this didn't work for Adam, and it won't work for you either.

b. Next, you may try comparison. I'm no worse than the next guy. But then you see the holiness of God and realize that both you and the "next guy" stand self-condemned.

c. Third on the list of self-help efforts that you and I drag out is a raft of religious chores. I'll pray more, I'll read the Bible through, I'll tithe—and give $100 to missions besides. I'll even go to Wednesday night services—the list goes on and on. But sooner or later we realize the stupidity of trying to bribe the Judge.

d. Then we make promises. We see Christ's five bleeding wounds as He hangs on the tree of crucifixion, and it sinks in on us that our sins put Him there. So we start promising. "I'll make it up to You, Jesus. I know I put You there, but I'll make it up to You; You'll see. I'll slave and serve and starve on the most primitive mission field. I'll take the most difficult assignments; I'll make it up to You. I'll even go to Nazarene Theological Seminary."

e. Then we fall into despair. All the brands of self-justification we have tried have turned into the ashes of absurdity. There is nothing else to do. We are up against the granite truth that there is absolutely nothing we can do to earn God's saving favor. And then we learn that we don't have to. In despair, defenses forsaken, we cry out, "O God, have mercy on me, a helpless, guilty sinner." And then the miracle comes.

It is a miracle well symbolized in James Stewart's story of the Faust painting. Faust, in the old story, gambled with his soul. An artist has painted the picture—a game of chess with Faust at one side, Satan at the other. The game in the picture is almost over, and Faust has only a few pieces left—a king, a knight, one or two pawns; and on his face there is a look of blank despair. On the other side of the board the devil leers in anticipation of his coming triumph. Many a chess player has looked at the picture and agreed that the position is hopeless; it is checkmate. But one day in the picture gallery a great master of the game stood gazing at the picture. He was fascinated by the look of terrible despair on the face of Faust. Then his gaze went to the pieces on the board. He stared at them absorbed. Other visitors in the gallery came and went, and still he studied the board, lost in contemplation. And then suddenly the gallery was startled by a ringing shout: "It is a lie! The king has another move! . . . *The king has another move!"*

I stand in that hall of justice, as guilty as sin condemned, hopeless, despairing. The sentence seems inevitable. I confess my miserable sins before the court. Suddenly a voice rings out, "The King has another move! The King of Kings has another move!" Jesus slips in and quietly stands by my side, and in a voice as calm as a silent sea and as deep as all eternity He says, "I became sin for him."

Miracle of miracles, the court proceedings change from prosecution of a transgressor to a joyous adoption proceeding.

This miracle comes when we obey the counsel of 1 John 1:9. "If we confess our sins, he is faithful and just to forgive us

44

our sins." And in that moment we understand John's words in chapter 4, verse 16, "So we . . . believe the love God has for us" (RSV).

2. But not only has God done something miraculous *for* us, He wants to do something marvelous *in* us

Read with me this second "ring of truth."

"The blood of Jesus Christ his Son cleanseth us from all sin" (1:7).

Further,

"He is faithful . . . to cleanse us from all unrighteousness" (v. 9, NIV).

And completing the ring, we find that the newly justified child is to dwell in God and God in him, for "he hath given us of his Spirit" (4:13), and "God dwelleth in us, and his love is perfected in us" (v. 12).

Studying this ring of truth, I see that what God wants to do *in* me has to do with

a. The indwelling Spirit

b. Perfect love

c. Cleansing from all sin

If time and your capacity for endurance permitted, I would like to speak to each of the three dimensions of what God wants to do *in* us. But I shall confine my remarks to only the third one, cleansing from all sin.

I do not wish to imply that in justification, regeneration, and adoption God does nothing within us. But I do want to emphasize the inward focus of this ring of truth. It is easy enough for converts to stop with the miracle of justification and fail to move on to entire sanctification. The early Wesleyan preachers were constantly, it seems, admonishing their hearers to go beyond what God had done *for* them and to open their hearts to the cleansing God wanted to do *in* them. For even the justified person will find within himself or herself what Adam Clarke

45

called "a foeman's heart." He or she will encounter a Romans 7 type of struggle.

Then Isa. 64:6 becomes remarkably self-descriptive: "We are all . . . unclean . . . we all do fade as a leaf; and our iniquities, like the wind, have taken us away." The prayer of Mic. 7:19 for God to "subdue our iniquities" becomes totally appropriate for the justified child of God. That word "iniquity" *(avon)* generally signifies an inner perversity.

And, sure enough, the newly justified child of God finds within himself a perversity that breaks his heart and threatens to blow him away like a maple leaf before an October wind. He cries out, "Who shall deliver me from the body of this death?"

And in spite of some very religious people who tell him that he is required to carry the seed of the serpent in his heart all life long, he reads today's text and discovers that inward sin, far from being necessary, is forbidden. Further, its cleansing is patently promised: "He is faithful . . . to cleanse us from all unrighteousness. . . . and the blood of Jesus Christ his Son cleanseth us from all sin."

The surrendered heart of the believer is cleansed from sin through the agency of Christ's Holy Spirit who comes to dwell in fullness, perfecting love in us.

God has done something miraculous *for* us. He has justified us freely. He has done something marvelous *in* us. He has sanctified us wholly. But I see still another matching ring of truth:

3. God wants to do something redemptive *through* us

Listen to this cyclical concert of truth:

"He that saith he abideth in him ought . . . to walk, even as he walked" (2:6).

"If God so loved us, we ought also to love one another" (4:11).

"This commandment have we from him, That he who loveth God love his brother also" (4:21).

46

And from the Gospel of John: "As my Father hath sent me, even so send I you" (20:21).

And completing the ring: "He laid down his life for us: and we ought to lay down our lives for the brethren" (1 John 3:16).

The one *for* whom God has done so much, and *in* whom God has wrought such a marvelous thing must now become a channel *through* which Christ can minister to the souls and bodies of people everywhere.

I salute you for answering the call of God to service. I think you know it is not a call to pamper yourself, seek special privileges, become rich, successful, or even happy. I think, don't you, that Jesus wants to lay down His life again through you and me.

Many arenas of service open before us. Millions live Christless lives of not-so-quiet desperation. I cannot prescribe your sacrifices or service. But God will guide you into redemptive service. Some of you may need to minister within your own family. Each family needs listeners, encouragers, and forgetters. Yes, forgetters. Some recent studies about why middle-aged people are divorcing show that many times it's because a spouse cannot forget. One man said, "When I was a young husband, I made mistakes, financial mistakes, career mistakes—and a romantic one. My wife could never let me forget a single one of them. My new wife doesn't even know about them. It's like getting set free from jail." Does your family need a "forgetter"?

Your church offers you many opportunities. One of the most rewarding things that happened to me in the last year was getting to sit in on some sessions where seminary students were teaching Cambodian refugees how to speak English. They had found another way to model Christ's love.

There is so much suffering that cries out for healing in Christ's name. Robert Coles studied the drawings of thousands of schoolchildren. He discovered that when white kids drew pictures of white children they drew neat, complete, whole pictures. When they drew pictures of black children, they drew incomplete pictures. They left off a foot or a hand, an eye or an ear, and many times they gave them inhuman faces that looked like monkeys or dogs.

On the other hand, when the black children drew pictures of whites, they too drew neat, complete, whole pictures. When the *black* children drew pictures of *black* children, they too drew incomplete pictures. They left off a foot or a hand, an eye or an ear. And, many times, they too gave them inhuman faces that looked like monkeys or dogs.

There is so much healing to be done in Christ's name.

> *True freedom is to share*
> *All the chains our neighbors wear,*
> *And, with heart and hand, to be*
> *Earnest to make others free.*
> —JAMES RUSSELL LOWELL

The life of holiness is a life of service. In the light of the *miraculous* thing God has done *for* us, and the *marvelous* thing He has done *in* us, let us spare no effort to let Him do something redemptive *through* us.

Here we have John's three rings of truth. The three form a matched set. Any ring missing from the set makes the other two incongruous, even ludicrous.

5

● **Paul Merritt Bassett**

"We, even we" are the very dwelling place of God. Scrub away the wrong and enthrone the perfectly right

Another Species

TEXT: 2 Cor. 6:14—7:1

We Christians have a strange understanding of human nature. On the one hand, we are utter and absolute pessimists about human nature—what it is and what it will do—apart from the grace of God, or rejecting the grace of God. Fine things will be said and done, to be sure, in the name of altruism or of some ideal. But we Christians believe that behind the altruism, behind the fine ideal, lies egotism and selfishness, and we are not surprised by those frequent outbreaks of human nastiness of which the media tell us and which we experience personally day to day. On the other hand we are utter and absolute optimists concerning what human nature can do and be when set upon by the grace of God.

It is to this very point that the apostle Paul addresses himself in our text:

Paul Merritt Bassett
Professor of the History of Christianity

49

Do not be yoked together with unbelievers. For what do righteousness and wickedness have in common? Or what fellowship can light have with darkness? What harmony is there between Christ and Belial? What does a believer have in common with an unbeliever? What agreement is there between the temple of God and idols? For we are the temple of the living God. As God has said:

"I will live with them and walk among them,
   and I will be their God,
   and they will be my people."
"Therefore come out from them
   and be separate,

says the Lord.

Touch no unclean thing,
   and I will receive you."
"I will be a Father to you,
   and you will be my sons and daughters,

says the Lord Almighty."

Since we have these promises, dear friends, let us purify ourselves from everything that contaminates body and spirit, perfecting holiness out of reverence for God *(2 Cor. 6:14—7:1, NIV)*.

Behind all that the apostle Paul says in this passage lies a very profound and very grand conviction—it is a conviction written across many a page in our Bibles, and it was a conviction spoken often by Jesus our Lord. We know it well, but its implications are so stunning that practicing it seems impossible. It is the conviction that "the heathen belong to one species, Chris-

---

"Another Species" by Paul Merritt Bassett is a classical example of proper exposition. The burdens follow sequentially, flowing from position to position with transitions, which climax in 2 Cor. 7:1, in getting "rid of the wrong" and attaining the "perfectly right." The sermon is an excellent example of allowing the passage to speak for itself. The holiness theme is apparent, with no extraneous language foreign to the passage being proclaimed.

tians to quite another" (Alfred Plummer, "Corinthians," *International Critical Commentary,* p. 203). So great are the differences between worldling and Christian that they must be accounted as of totally separate parentage; their similarities are only superficial. This is quite a conviction, is it not?

Out of this conviction, then, Paul admonishes the Corinthian Christians: "Do not tie up with unbelievers." He exhorts, "Don't climb in the yoke with infidels." Then Paul raises a series of questions designed to show just how impossible it is to be bound with the faithless.

What partnership can righteousness have with unrighteousness? When it comes to how and why we do what we do, Christians and unbelievers are incompatible from the word "go." "Our citizenship is in heaven," says Paul in another place (Phil. 3:20, NIV).

What fellowship have light and darkness? At the point of what we believe true knowledge and understanding are, Christians and unbelievers work from essentially different, even contradictory, definitions. As Paul says in another place: "Whatever gain was mine, I chalked it off as loss for Christ's sake. In fact, I chalk off everything as loss because of the incalculable value of knowing Christ Jesus my Lord. For his sake I suffer losing everything. . . . That I may know him and the power of his resurrection and partnership in his sufferings, becoming like him in his death, so that if possible I may attain the resurrection from the dead" (Phil. 3:8, 10-11, author's translation).

What harmony can there be between Christ and the prince of devils? At the point of who is lord of one's life, Christians and unbelievers sing very different hymns of praise. As Paul says to the Thessalonians: "The mystery of lawlessness is already working. . . . And the lawless one will be revealed for what he is, and the Lord Jesus will slay him with the mere breath of his mouth and destroy him by appearing and coming. The coming of the lawless one will be fraught with power and apparent signs and wonders, and with totally unconscionable deception for those who are to perish for their refusal to love the truth and so to be saved. Such is the activity of Satan. . . . But we are bound to give thanks to God always . . . because God chose you in the first place to be saved, through sanctification of spirit and belief in the truth. And here is that to which he calls you through our gospel: the obtaining of the glory of our Lord Jesus Christ" (2 Thess. 2:7-14, author's paraphrase).

What common ground is there between believers and unbelievers? At the point of who we are at the very root of our being, Christians and unbelievers take their identities from absolutely different sources.

What similarity is there between the temple of the living God, where God is worshipped without human handmade representation, and those idols with their splendid shrines? At the point of knowing who is real and where reality is, Christians and unbelievers look in entirely opposing directions. We do not come to a God who abides only in the church building. In a profound sense, we bring Him into this building with us. If we do not find Him here, it is because we do not find Him dwelling in us.

Christians are of a different species from the rest of the human race. Any similarities are superficial: for the way we determine right and wrong, the way we think, the principles out of which we live, our understanding of ourselves, our understanding of the world—all is transformed for the sake of the new species.

Paul then brings this part of his thinking to a climax with as rousing a declaration—and one as hard to believe—as could be made by a human being. English translations miss the emphatic character of it here: "We, even we," says Paul (even we Corinthians viewed by all the world as given over to obsessions with alcohol and sex), "We, even we are now just what God says we are. We are temples of the living God." And not just temples in some vague sense. Paul has no interest in telling them that God's presence in us is some nebulous "good feeling" or "tingling power." Theirs it is not to be *barely* or *generally* temples. The word which Paul uses indicates the very sanctuary, the very dwelling place of God, a very specific and personal place. They have been made by God into the *naos,* His holy of holies, the most sacred precinct of all.

In Paul's world, the *naos* was the little cell or niche in the Greek temples in which the image of the god was placed. However grand the rest of the building, here in the *naos* was "what it was all about." Now, says Paul, you Corinthians are that niche. Not for them the status of being rather remote and accidental hosts of our God—reflectors of some distant glory, reminiscences or sparks of a faraway divinity. They are the *naos* of God—the niche is in them by design. They are His shrine. They are sacred precincts, holy places, the sanctuary. And what likeness can there be between those who are the very sanctuary of Almighty God and those whose emptiness leads them to human-made niches where stand or sit the gods made with hands?

But what kind of God inhabits such a sanctuary? Paul lets God speak for himself. And this God who inhabits human sanctuaries makes some promises. He will be a *living* God; He will set up house, as it were, in human beings; He will take them in, He will welcome them; and He will be Father to them. Is there a type of progression here? For God to be a *living* God would be for Him to be far grander than the lifeless chunks of stone and carved logs that made gods then—and better, too, than the windy mottoes, and trendy things, and sex goddesses and gods (who seemed finally to age and disappear anyway) that crowd our pantheons these days. Just to have a *living* God—there is comfort in that. At least someone is in charge in the universe! Even in Corinth.

But more than living, He makes His home in them. To be sure, He is transcendent and He is almighty. But how marvelous that such a God should say, as He himself has said, "I will make

53

my home in them!" How they needed that presence! And yet strangers, or hired help, or third cousins, either people or ideas or things—even the people of God, or ideas about God, or things of God—can set up house in us, can take us over and rule our roost. But our God turns the metaphor: "I will set up my home there, but they are welcome! When I, the living God, come to set up house in them, it will be as father, and it will transform them into sons and daughters."

Then the apostle, perhaps realizing how incredible these things must sound, especially to the likes of the Corinthians, nails the credibility down in unmistakable terms: he adds, "This is by *o kurios pantokratōr*—this is the word of the Lord who rules over everything, who has the power to bring it to pass."

"Having these promises, then," says Paul, "let us prepare for their full realization in us." For this preparation there is both a negative process and a positive process. "Having promises like these, and already being the *naos* of the living God, let us scrub completely away every kind of defilement, every stain, every pollutant, every thing that may contribute to the development of a wallowing place in us, whether it be a matter of flesh or of spirit. Let us flush it out!" And why not? Just reflect on who has promised to live there—and reflect too on the switch in metaphor, for He invites us to live there as well. He does not live in the wallow, nor need we. That's the negative side: Scrub away any inclination to compromise! Get rid of the wrong!

And, "having promises like these, perfect holiness." The negative is hardly enough. Only scrubbing away the defilement can lead to the worst sorts of spiritual pride and lovelessness, to presumption and other deadly maladies of spirit. Jesus said that there is that kind of person who sweeps the house clean of evil, and fills it with nothing good, and to that house return the demons sevenfold. And the end of that person is worse than the beginning. So now the apostle calls for us to do what appears to be impossible, impossible because the basic resources that he assumes are there may not be there, and impossible because even if the resources were there, it's a matter of going beyond an absolute limit, exceeding a proven maximum. Look at that phrase of the apostle's again: perfect holiness—bring holiness to completion! (Here we see the sense of the NIV translation, and we see also the sense of the KJV and the RSV.) Develop sanctity to fulfillment! To the limit of capacity! That's the positive side: Complete your sanctity! Attain the perfectly right!

Get rid of the wrong; attain the perfectly right—but not merely in the love of human beings nor in the fear of human beings. Get rid of the wrong; attain the perfectly right— but not in any way from some fear of evaluation or judgment of human beings. Get rid of the wrong; attain the perfectly right and good and true in *"the fear of God."* It is the holy God who makes the final assessment—and in the run of an authentic life, His assessment, though it may be made through His people, is the only assessment that counts.

But how do we keep all of this from being merely human enterprise? An exercise in some sort of human main strength and awkwardness? Paul has already given us the clues:

1. We are already God's *naos:* "We, yes we, *are* a sanctuary of the living God" (Plummer's translation, p. 202). Paul speaks of the *church* here. The church, as the congregation of believers, is the *naos* of God. He is addressing his "beloved," his dear brothers and sisters in Christ. This is not evangelism, not missions, not declaration to the lost. Here is a word to the church, those already become the sanctuary of the living God—the inner sanctum of the living God. And Paul has made it abundantly clear how this has come about. In fact, he had just said it, a few verses earlier: "Christ died for all, that those who live should no longer live for themselves, but for him who died for them and was raised again. . . . Therefore if anyone be in Christ, he is a new creature. . . . All of this is from God, who reconciled us to himself through Christ. . . . God made him who knew no sin to be sin for

us, so that through him we might become the righteousness of God" (2 Cor. 5:15, 17-18, 21, author's paraphrase).

Here, then, is our first clue as to how getting rid of the wrong and attaining the perfectly right is to be kept clear of mere human striving. It is God in Christ who has created holiness and given it to us. We only cultivate it. But we cultivate it. Are we cultivating what is honorable, just, pure, lovely, and gracious?

2. And the second clue as to how getting rid of the wrong and attaining the perfectly right is to be kept clear of mere human striving is in Paul's insistence that we do have the promises of the Father. We have them. They are ours. And truly to have promises from God, the all-ruling Lord—*o kurios pantokratōr*—is to rest assured in their fulfillment. They are now as good as done! In fact, Paul says, in Christ they *are* done. They are fulfilled, they are realized. For, says the writer of the Revelation, Christ is God the Father's great "Amen," and Paul began this letter saying: "No matter how many promises God has made, they are 'yes' (i.e., 'amen'—'so be it') in Christ." And at other times, too, he says that Christ is God's great "so be it" to the promises—to all of them.

3. So here is our third clue as to how getting rid of the wrong and attaining the perfectly right is to be kept clear of human striving. It is openness to letting God (who in Christ has fulfilled His precious promises) fulfill them right here in us and among us. He initiates, we respond; He creates, we cultivate; He promises, we purge and perfect that the promises may be fulfilled.

We Christians are of a different species. Our ethics are radically different from those of the world. What can unqualified love of neighbor and even of enemy have in common with self-interest and egocentrism? Our pursuit of knowledge, our yearning to understand, is essentially irreconcilable with that of the world. So what fellowship can knowing and understanding for Christ's sake and for the sake of others have with knowing and understanding for the sake of impressing and for the sake of climbing earthly ladders to status? Our allegiance, our fundamental commitment, is our very selves, from peak of roof to foundation; it is totally contrary to the world's commitment and allegiance.

So what harmony can there be between living for Christ, who served and plainly gave all for us, and living for Belial, who serves only self and is father of deceit? Our very identities are from the very root totally different from those of the worldling. So what can we believers have in common with infidels? And our convictions about who reality is and where reality is are completely out of square with the world's perceptions. So how can we live as homes for idols when such places are totally incongruent with the temple of God?

So radically different are we that we are sanctuaries for the living God. And being sanctuaries for the living God, we are radically different. We are the sanctuaries-of-the-living-God species. "We, even we!" says Paul. And not just "sometime" homes for a traveling deity either. We are right where He really lives—not mere praisers of God, not mere sacrificers to God, not mere onlookers to holy activity, not mere hearers of marvelous words. We are His very niches, His shrines, His holy places. *We, even we!*

And if this grand "we, even we!" is truly ours, then we have "great and precious promises"—now already fulfilled in us by Christ's presence here. The presence of the living God who creates no strangers, who makes no third cousins, but who relates to us only as a father to children is enshrined within us. And if the beginning of the fulfillment of these promises be so glorious as we know it to be even now, what must be the end of the story?

If we know the beginning of the story, how profoundly moved we are to open our house to that glorious finale! Many a guest has passed through my home in my lifetime, and I have tried to be a gracious host. But no matter how gracious I have been, not one of those guests has proposed to adopt me. None except this one, who came to my real house, the one that only He could see. And He said, "I will live even here! Be my child!" Then comes the other side of the metaphor: I have been a guest, even sometimes a very welcome guest, but never has my host, no matter how famously we got along, said to me, "Would you consider adoption? Be my child!" But the living God has come to me and has said, "I will live with you and walk with you and I will be your God, and you shall be my child. Therefore come out from the world and be separate, touch no unclean thing, and I will receive you. I will be a father to you, and you shall be my child, says the Lord Almighty."

Having such promises as these, knowing what Christ has done for us and is doing in us, as an earnest of the future, we will not want the slightest blemish on the integrity of our relationship to Him or to others or to His world. And beyond that, we yearn to bring the glorious process to fulfillment: "Since we have these promises, dear friends, let us purify ourselves from everything that contaminates body and spirit, and let us perfect holiness in the fear of God." Amen.

6

● **Oscar F. Reed**

*Christian holiness is about
the long journey
from dependence to interdependence*

Holiness—A Christian Paradox

TEXT: *For though I am free from all men, I have made myself a slave to all, that I might win the more* (1 Cor. 9:19, RSV).

This great passage is a Christian paradox. "I am free . . . I am a slave." But it is more than a paradox. It is the climax of chapters 8—10 where Paul elevates the law of love above the law of liberty. The three chapters present a window into the mind and heart of a great soul.

Here is a "noble heart" who writes with deep emotion and tender winsomeness; a church leader who boldly reveals his heart before the people he loves.

The movement of the passage is from self-realization to renunciation and self-discipline for the sake of others. It is the pilgrimage of a great pastor. It is the story of a man who moves

Oscar F. Reed
Professor of Preaching

from
    dependence
        to independence
            to interdependence.
From the idea of contract to covenant fellowship.

Let us follow that pilgrimage with Paul and bring his story to our story.

"I am free" indicates there was a time when Paul was not free. Will you allow me to call this bondage a spirit of *dependence.*

Paul was a "Pharisee of the Pharisees," obedient to the Mosaic law and restricted by the multitude of Jewish fences. He "consented" to Stephen's death and persecuted the Christians. He became the "hatchet man" of the high priest, ferreting out the followers of Jesus and bringing them to trial. His zeal made him the scourge of all who followed the Master.

Dependence meant a bondage to
    religion
        law
            state
                culture
                    synagogue
                        Temple
Dependence ended in
    fear
        insecurity
            and anxiety.
It always does!

———————

The sermon, "Holiness—A Christian Paradox," by Oscar F. Reed, develops a textual inferential message from 1 Cor. 9:19, using the whole chapter as supporting collateral for the three main burdens. It might be noted that Dr. Reed brought an obvious holiness theme to a passage which in and of itself does not use holiness vocabulary.

And then Paul heard the voice of Jesus on the road to Damascus, and the chains of dependence fell off in a freedom he had dreamed of but never experienced. Filled with the Spirit, he burst into the streets of that Syrian city and proclaimed in the synagogue that Jesus was the "Son of God." No wonder he could exultantly cry out to the Corinthians, "I am free."

The grace of God is always like that. It frees us from so many chains that make us less than what we ought to be. We are not truly human until Jesus delivers us from the old life to the richness of our new life in Him.

Would you allow me to suggest that Paul moved from *dependence* to *interdependence?* He progressed from duress under law to freedom under grace.

He had met Jesus! He was free of the Pharisees. Free from the bondage of law, home, and synagogue. *Free to allow grace to have its way.* How good it must have felt, at last—at long last—"I am free."

The long days in Arabia, however, introduced a new dimension that the apostle at first had not seen. It was troubling to believe that his *independence* under grace would turn back to *dependence* unless he moved on to *interdependence*.

There are thousands of young people in the Americas who believe themselves to be free but who are really not free—dependent rather than independent.

I watched the "street people" of Berkeley, Calif. Leaving homes from Toronto to San Francisco, they represented a generation of youth who declared their independence only to find themselves enslaved to their own passions, alcohol, and drugs. Their pseudoindependence rejected a spirit of dependence.

One day on the university mall a young bearded student preached the gospel to a score of street people under the influence of drugs. I could not understand why he preached—they were not hearing. Or at least I thought they were not hearing.

"I was one of them," said a student to me.

"Why does he preach?" I replied.

"Because, like me, there are those who believe and are saved. They took me to their hostel, cleaned me up, and secured me a job. I learned what it meant to be a disciple of Jesus. We are waiting for His coming and preparing for the persecution which will accompany that Advent."

I replied, "But I am a Christian too."

"I knew that," he said. "That is why I spoke to you."

Independence can only lead to dependence unless, under the sanctifying grace of God, Christ's followers move on to *interdependence*. "I am free . . . but I have made myself a slave to win the more."

"Am I not free?

"Am I not an apostle?

"Have I not seen Jesus our Lord?

"Are not you my workmanship . . . ?" (1 Cor. 9:1, RSV).

Then why not insist on my rights? Because I am a love-slave of Jesus Christ. I have no rights. My ministry is my own reward.

Thus, Paul became "all things to all men" through a spirit of holy accommodation—a depth of *interdependence*, if you please.

Paul became as a Jew to win Jews. In Lystra he insisted on the circumcision of Timothy to identify with those "under the law." According to Jewish custom, he took a vow before going to Jerusalem. While in the holy city he paid the fees of a Nazirite group who were released from their vows at the Temple.

None of this was necessary. But Paul understood that personal identification with those "under the law" was of superlative importance in winning them to Christ.

The apostle became as "one outside the law," though under the law of Christ, to win the pagans to the Lord. He was not lawless, but he argued from their own grounds, quoted from their own poetry, and proclaimed the "unknown God" at the Acropolis in Athens as the true God and Father of Jesus Christ.

To the weak Paul became weak . . . "that I might win the weak." The eating of meat offered to idols means nothing to us, but the ethical principle is still present. Paul would not enter the pagan temple because of its associations with idol worship and concluded, "Therefore if food is a cause of my brother's falling, I will never eat meat lest I cause my brother to fall."

"Must my conscience be bound by another's?" asked Paul. "No, my greatest liberty is in identifying with another in order to lead him to Christ." He was a servant, the *doulos* of Jesus. His was a spirit of *interdependence*. He must take his place with all men under the law of Christ.

While at a beautiful restaurant in San Francisco, a young lawyer looked across the table at me and said, "Dr. Reed, play golf with us in the morning. We tee off in the Oakland hills at 6 a.m."

Six a.m., I thought! It was already 10:30 at night, and it would be 2 a.m. before we could cross the bay to Oakland and go to bed after the scheduled tour of the city. And then a voice said, "Oscar, you play golf with those two young men!"

Obedient to that inner impulse, I breakfasted with John and Allen near Lake Merritt and teed off into dense fog at 6 a.m. They later said that I didn't wake up until the ninth hole. But you know, a lawyer and a young contractor found Christ. It was the interest in and identity with these men that made the difference.

In verses 24-27 Paul gets so excited about the prospects of his love relation with Christ that his theology becomes poetry. He mixes his metaphors but soars to great truths. He is interested in all of us winning an imperishable wreath and disciplining ourselves so we will not be disqualified in the end.

Paul was so sold out to Christ that he would endure anything rather than put an obstacle in the way of the gospel of Christ. At every point he identified himself with others.

Some of you know the exultant cry of freedom and enjoy the spirit of *independence*, "I am free!" However, freedom is not freedom unless it is found in slavery to another for one reason—that I might win some to Jesus Christ—that is, a spirit of *interdependence*.

Isn't that what Christian holiness is all about? The sanctifying grace of Jesus Christ brings us from *independence* to *interdependence*. No wonder we can say with Paul, "I am free, but I have become a slave to all that I might win some to Christ."

7

• **Rob L. Staples**

*The life of holiness is inseparable from
the utterly incomprehensible condescension
modeled by Jesus Christ*

The Disposition of Discipleship

SCRIPTURE: Matt. 16:24; Phil. 2:5-11

Just what does it mean to
be a disciple of Jesus? In considering that question, let us examine some words of Jesus and some words of Paul. The words of Jesus are recorded in Matt. 16:24—"Then Jesus told his disciples, 'If any man would come after me, let him deny himself and take up his cross and follow me'" (RSV).* The words of Paul are found in Phil. 2:5-11, the famous so-called kenosis passage— "Have this mind among yourselves, which is yours in Christ Jesus, who, though he was in the form of God, did not count equality with God a thing to be grasped, but emptied himself, taking the form of a servant, being born in the likeness of men.

---

*Unless otherwise indicated, all Scripture quotations in this sermon are from the *Revised Standard Version*.

Rob L. Staples
Professor of Theology

And being found in human form he humbled himself and became obedient unto death, even death on a cross. Therefore God has highly exalted him and bestowed on him the name which is above every name, that at the name of Jesus every knee should bow, in heaven and on earth and under the earth, and every tongue confess that Jesus Christ is Lord, to the glory of God the Father."

Paul is writing about unity in the church, encouraging the Christians at Philippi to avoid selfishness and to "count others better than themselves" (v. 3). In order to show them the meaning of unity in the church, he points them to the Head of the Church, Christ Jesus. In verses 6-11, he quotes what some think is an early Christian hymn, either written by Paul himself at an earlier date or adapted by him from some other source. He uses this hymn to tell them that they are to have "the mind of Christ" among them—not "in" them as the King James Version has it, not "in" each person individually and subjectively, but "among" them, relationally and corporately, as a community that has its basis "in Christ Jesus."

The word "mind" here does not mean intelligence or reason, but "mindedness," "mind-set," "attitude," or "disposition." I like the translation of verse 5 by the New Testament scholar, F. W. Beare: "Let this be the disposition that governs in your common life, as is fitting in Christ Jesus." From this translation I have taken the theme for this message, "The Disposition of Discipleship." If we can understand this "disposition of discipleship,"

Two critical passages from Matthew and Philippians are used by Rob L. Staples in his beautiful exposition of the kenosis passage from Philippians. It will be interesting to the reader to see how Dr. Staples turns to Matt. 16:24 to identify the "disposition of discipleship" as the heart of holiness. Here is movement from one passage to a second in order to concretize the application for the hearers.

we will understand the substance of Christian holiness, even though none of the typical "Wesleyan" terms appear in the passage.

Paul tells us three things which constitute our Lord's "disposition" as He fulfilled His redemptive mission. These same three things, urges the apostle, are to constitute the disposition of anyone who would be Christ's disciple.

1. As Paul points us to Christ, the first thing he mentions is His voluntary selflessness

"Christ Jesus," says Paul, "though he was in the form of God, did not count equality with God a thing to be grasped, but emptied himself, taking the form of a servant, being born in the likeness of men."

Theologians have debated whether Paul is referring to the self-emptying of the preexistent Christ or of the incarnate Christ. Does the self-emptying occur as Christ leaves heaven to come to earth, or does self-emptying characterize His life while on earth? Although Paul believed in Christ's preexistence, the grammar here points to the latter interpretation. He emptied himself, "taking" or "having taken" the form of a servant. Having become a man, He went about on earth living a self-emptying life. And this is *our* Pattern. We are to "let [his] be the disposition that governs in [our] common life, as is fitting in Christ Jesus."

He was in "the form of God." As Karl Barth says, "He was God's Equal." But He did not consider this equality a thing to be grasped. The contrast with the first Adam is obvious. In the Garden of Eden, Adam *did* grasp for equality with God. In essence he said: "Not thy will, but mine, be done." But in another Garden called Gethsemane, our soul-sorrowing and blood-sweating Lord prayed: "Not my will, but thine, be done" (Luke 22:42). He who was "in the form of God" resisted the temptation to hold onto that form. This was the same temptation with which Satan had confronted Him at the beginning of His ministry

67

(see Matt. 4:1-11), a temptation to at least *look* a little more like God, to keep "in top form," the "form of God." But He resisted. He emptied himself.

Another theological question arises here: Of what did He empty himself? A product of 19th-century liberal theology was the so-called kenosis theory, which said that when Christ left heaven He laid aside His divine attributes, so that while on earth He was fully and only a man. But although the theory took its name from Paul's word in verse 7 (*ekenōsen*—"emptied") and although its intention may have been good, it nevertheless makes a separation between the Persons of the Godhead which Christian faith cannot tolerate. And it does so by taking Paul's poetic religious language and turning it into a speculative, rational theory.

The simplest solutions are often the best, and it seems best here to understand Paul as meaning that Christ emptied himself "of himself." That is, He just gave himself away to others. In the words of Isa. 53:12, "He poured out his soul to death." And in the words of Dietrich Bonhoeffer, he became "a man for others." This is the mind-set which we should have, says Paul. We are to let this be the disposition that governs in our common life.

Our Lord's self-emptying was completely *voluntary.* He emptied *himself.* He *took upon himself* the servant-form. No blind fate forced it upon Him. Not even His Heavenly Father forced it upon Him. He himself willed it so. In sovereign freedom He puts off the form of God and takes on the appearance of a servant, the appearance of a being that is not God. What we then see is the form of a man, the form of one exposed to all the dubiousness, ambiguity, and darkness of the human situation. We see the *form* not of a Lord but of a servant.

Now let us turn to the parallel text in Matt. 16:24: "Jesus told his disciples, 'If any man would come after me, let him *deny himself.*'" This self-denial to which Jesus calls us is not unlike the self-emptying of which Paul speaks in Philippians. It is more than merely making a few sacrifices and putting up with a few inconveniences. It is more than giving up meat on Fridays and throughout Lent, although there may be spiritual value in that. It is more than giving up a new Easter outfit in order to put more money in the missionary offering, although there is certainly spiritual value in that. When Jesus calls His disciples to self-denial, He is telling them they must give themselves up, pour themselves out, subordinate themselves and become servants, be done with self-centeredness, letting self no longer be sovereign but subservient both to the will of God and to the needs of humanity. It is in echoing the thought of his Master that Paul says, "Let this be the disposition that governs in your common life"—voluntary selflessness.

2. The second thing about Christ to which Paul points us is His vicarious suffering

The Christ who in verse 7 is said to have "emptied himself" is said in verse 8 to have "humbled himself." "Being found in human form he humbled himself and became obedient unto death, even death on a cross."

Let us look immediately to the parallel text in Matt. 16:24—"Jesus told his disciples, 'If any man would come after me, let him deny himself and *take up his cross.'*"

Christ's death was a full atonement for our sins. No other sacrifice is needed. Therefore He does not ask us to take up His cross and help Him bear it. He bore it all alone.

> *His blood atones for all our race*
> *And sprinkles now the throne of grace.*

But He calls on us to take up *our* cross. Crosses are not mere *burdens*. Living in this house of clay, we bear many burdens which are a part of this natural order, the "thousand natural shocks that flesh is heir to," as Shakespeare makes Hamlet say. But a cross is *someone else's burden*. Christ asks His disciples to decide to suffer vicariously in solidarity with suffering humanity.

69

Now and then we see glimpses of this among fellow Christians. My friend and colleague, the late Dr. James McGraw, once said to me: "When my son was dying with cancer a few years ago, my pastor came to the hospital night after night and sat with me hour after hour. He was a good pastor. He never tried to explain to me why it had to happen. He never tried to solve the problem of natural evil. *He just cried with me.*" That is a glimpse of vicarious suffering; perhaps it isn't the whole picture.

When Paul says that Christ Jesus became "obedient unto death," what does he mean? To whom, or to what, did he become obedient? The apostle does not say. Certainly Christ's obedience was to God. But it may be that Paul is reflecting on our Lord's submission to the very power of death that reigns over the human situation. He says in Rom. 6:16: "If you yield yourselves to any one as obedient slaves, you are slaves of the one whom you obey." A slave must be obedient to the one to whom he is committed. And in taking on the form of a slave, Jesus committed himself to the human condition. And that human condition finds its common denominator in the fact of death.

That being the case, to "take up our cross" may mean more than weeping with those who weep. It may mean to "die daily" with those who die. Mother Teresa of Calcutta, who was awarded the Nobel peace prize a few years ago, has given her life to minister to the sick, the diseased, the "wretched refuse" of Calcutta's streets, the "huddled masses" who know not the meaning of freedom from want. Moving among those suffering people, giving a cup of water or a piece of bread, or laying a hand on a fevered brow; moving among those poor, despised creatures, breathing the contagion of their diseases into her own body, she ministers to human need at the daily risk of dying. "Taking up our cross" means more than offering our sympathy. It involves the willingness to lay down our lives, if need be, for the sake of the suffering and oppressed.

But there is still another dimension which must be considered if we are to get the full picture. Sometimes when Christ's disciples seek to minister to a world that is deathly sick (or even to a Church that has some serious ailments), they are rejected, misunderstood, sometimes crucified. Then they learn a little more about what it means to take up one's cross.

Later in this Epistle to the Philippians, Paul expresses his deep desire to "know him, and the power of his resurrection, and the fellowship of his sufferings" (3:10, KJV). At first glance we might think Paul's order should be reversed, that the power of the Resurrection should *follow* the fellowship of sufferings. But Paul, seeing a deeper dimension of discipleship, knows that it is only through the power of the Resurrection that we are enabled to enter into the fellowship of Christ's redemptive suffering. To really experience Easter is to become implicated in the cross-bearing of Good Friday. Vicarious suffering! He who is the Lord of the Church humbled himself, becoming obedient to death, even the death of the Cross. "Let this," says the apostle, "be the disposition that governs in your common life."

3. Paul speaks not only of Christ's voluntary selfishness, and His vicarious suffering, but also of His vindicated status

In verse 7, Christ *emptied* himself. In verse 8, He *humbled* himself. But in verse 9, *God* has exalted Him!

We can easily miss the meaning of verses 9-11. We miss their meaning if we see Christ's exaltation simply as His reward for a job well done, as a victory which comes at the *end* of a battle.

We must reject the notion that Christ received "the name which is above every name" as a reward for His humiliation. The exaltation is not a *sequel* to the humiliation. The sequence involved here is not at all like some home mission pastor struggling along sacrificially at Podunk and then finally being rewarded with a call to First Church!

What Paul is saying in verses 9-11 is that it is precisely just this humiliated Jesus who is now the Lord at God's right hand! Not a Christ who for a while became a servant, and then was promoted out of this servant role to that of Kingship. Rather it is the selfless One, the suffering One, the dying One—just Him—who is given the name that is above every name. As the Servant, just as the Servant, He *is* Lord.

When the ancient Christian artists painted Christ's ascension and enthronement, they left on His brow and in His hands the scars from the Cross. Not even the Resurrection erased those scars. That is the meaning of the word "therefore" in verse 9. It does not mean that He who was humbled and humiliated was *afterwards* exalted and thus rewarded for His self-denial and obedience. What it says is that precisely the One who was abased and humbled, even to the obedience of death on a cross, *is* the Lord. We are not to look at the picture of Christ's crucifixion and seek there for some other element, some other factor, and make that the basis of His exaltation.

There is no mention in this passage of Christ reassuming the "form of God" which He had laid aside. No, He who became man and was crucified, whose abasement and humiliation is by no means abandoned or cancelled; He, just He, is the One who is exalted. It is *to Him* that the great name is given; it is *of Him* that verses 9-11 are written. There is no other Christ than this—the Servant who is the Lord. It is as if there is now a new God-form, a new way to recognize the Redeemer. The name Lord now belongs to the abased and humbled One.

Now let us take a final look at Matt. 16:24—"Jesus told his disciples, 'If any man would come after me, let him deny himself and take up his cross and *follow me.*'" How are we to understand those words "follow me"? Surely they are not the same as "come after me" in the first part of the verse. It may help a little to know that "deny himself" and "take up his cross" are aorist active imperatives, while "follow me" is the present tense of continuous action. That may help a little, but in all due respect to the Greek, it doesn't help a great deal. But if the parallel which we have suggested between this verse and the kenosis passage in Philippians can be carried all the way through, then perhaps Jesus is calling us to follow Him into that realm of self-denial and vicarious suffering which is its own vindication and looks for no other reward!

In 1 Pet. 2:20, we read: "If when you do what is right and suffer for it you patiently endure it, that is grace *(charis)* with God" (NASB). As surely as we live, if we do what is right in this world, we will suffer for it. But if we endure it patiently, says Peter, that is "grace." But we get impatient. We long for victory and vindication, and we want it now. But Peter did not say that if we endure, then someday in some "beautiful isle of some-where" we will lay our burdens "down by the riverside." No, just to be engaged in the battle—muddied and bloodied and scarred in the fight for truth, for justice, for right—that is the victory! For we are in Christ Jesus. And in Christ Jesus the servant does not eventually get to be lord; the servant *is* lord!

And so the "disposition of discipleship" is nothing less than the commitment to follow Jesus into that Kingdom where sovereignty means servanthood, where being a victor means becoming a victim; to follow Him into that realm of self-emptying, suffering, and service into which He led the way—

—that realm of obedience unto death

—that realm where "the fellowship of suffering" does not precede but rather follows "the power of his resurrection"

—that realm where our Easter faith finds its expression in Good Friday sacrifice

—that realm where (to use Paul's imagery) we here on earth, along with those in heaven, and those under the earth, bow our knees to acknowledge and move our tongues to confess that the One whom God has made Lord is none other than the lowly Suffering Servant.

Into that realm, into that Kingdom, Jesus calls to His disciples: "Follow me." To enter that Kingdom is to enter the life of Christian holiness.

God has found His glory in this—that He, kenotically and incognito, prepares His kingdom in utterly incomprehensible condescension. Jesus, God's Equal, has found His name in this—that in the depth of His humiliation He is called "Lord." And the Church, the Body of Christ, finds both her name and her glory in this—that she, although existing as the "People of God," does not grasp for equality with God, does not seek to be God, but makes herself "of no reputation," empties herself, humbles herself, loses herself, takes "the form of a servant" and becomes obedient—obedient to the death, the death of the Cross.

8

• **Harvey E. Finley**

*Holiness has been God's standard for us
all along*

Holiness unto the Lord

SCRIPTURE: Lev. 19:1-4, 9-18; Matt. 5:43-48; Rom. 12:1-2

TEXTS: Lev. 19:2: *You shall be holy, for I the Lord your God am
holy;* Matt. 5:48: *Therefore you are to be perfect, as your
heavenly Father is perfect* (both NASB).*

The flag flying high at the top of the mast of a ship on the high seas identifies those flying it. A banner unfurled at the head of a group of demonstrators shouts the cause of those displaying it. In the world of religion there are those of us who gladly bear the banner "Holiness unto the Lord." We have a deep-seated concern to promote the cause of holiness. Thus those committed to "Holiness unto the Lord" have an underlying conviction that this is the only way to live if life is to be satisfying and fulfilling, and if there is ever to be a

---

*Unless otherwise indicated, all Scripture quotations in this sermon are from the *New American Standard Bible.*

Harvey E. Finley
Professor of Old Testament

suitable solution to social ills and evils. It is, as well, the only way to be properly prepared for life after death.

"Holiness unto the Lord" is a phrase which occurs in earlier English versions of the Bible, such as the Authorized Version of King James and the American Standard Version. It is to be compared with "Holy to the Lord" of recent versions, such as the *New American Standard Bible* and the *New International Version.* It is a phrase which highlights or emphasizes God's requirement of being holy, as set forth in our text. It conveys the meaning "to be set apart" unto or for the Lord. For human beings it also conveys the deeper meaning of having one's life touched and transformed by God so as to be able to live in conformity with His holy character and will. As we consider, then, how God's people are expected to meet the requirement, "You shall be holy," there are two points of reference concerning the holiness of God to which we must give our attention: first, the *wholly-otherness* of God; and second, the *moral perfection* of God.

1. "You shall be holy" in relation to the "wholly-otherness" of God

It may appear even before thinking about how the *wholly-otherness* of God relates to the holiness of God's people that there is little or no basis for any such consideration. The thought,

---

Our professor of Old Testament, Harvey E. Finley, has used selected exposition as his homiletical model in preaching from the subject "Holiness unto the Lord." Using several passages of scripture from both the Old and the New Testaments, he develops his theme directly from the passage, moving from the holiness of God to the imperative, "Ye shall be holy." He points out how the New Testament commandments find their foundations in the Old Testament, and he applies the material as a word for today. The call to holiness, then, is a call to a quality of life which our world desperately needs.

even truth, that God is *wholly other* in His essence or being in comparison with His creature "man" would seem to terminate any comment before it ever began.

God's Wholly-otherness. The Exodus 19 through Leviticus 9 context shows that the *wholly-other* aspect of God relates significantly to how the people of God are to meet the requirement of holiness. These considerations derive in particular from those instances when God revealed himself to Moses and His people in an awesome and mystifying manner.

God appeared to Moses in a flame that enveloped a bush but did not consume it. Moses was attracted to the bush, and as he drew near, God spoke to him: "Do not come near here; remove your sandals from your feet, for the place on which you are standing is holy ground" (Exod. 3:5).

God made known His presence in the midst of His people as a "pillar of cloud by day" and a "pillar of fire by night" during the days of journeying from Egypt to the Promised Land (Exod. 13:22; 40:38). He also appeared on Mount Sinai in a mysterious, ominous, awesome cloud which covered the top of the mountain as He gave the Law to Moses for Israel. The presence of God in the form of a flame enveloping the bush and of a *glory (kabod)-cloud* was the means whereby God, the *Wholly Other,* remained hidden as to the fullness of His divine Being and at the same time revealed himself in meaningful encounter with Moses and His people.

He thus is the God who is known and still not known. He is the One who grants His presence and still remains hidden. He is the One who has granted the most significant disclosures of himself to mankind in the Incarnation, the sending of His Son, and in bestowing the Gift of the Holy Spirit upon His Church. But still He has not totally disclosed His full glory. Herein is the mystery and majesty of our great and mighty God.

Further, God disclosed to Moses various stipulations in order for Israel to worship Him properly. He gave directions to Moses concerning a portable sanctuary (Exodus 26—27; 30; 35—38), a priesthood (Exodus 28—29; 39; Leviticus 8—9), and various sacrifices (Leviticus 1—7). These religious institutions were God's gracious gift to His people to provide an atonement for their sins and a daily renewal of their initial consecration to God in the covenant established at Sinai (Exod. 24:1-8). Thus in a sanctuary, priests, altar, and sacrifices, God the *Wholly Other* provided for the salvation of His people Israel. Stated differently, God the *Wholly Other* is the Author or Source of salvation; the wonderful provisions for redemption originate deep within the mysterious, incomprehensible Divine Being.

2. God's wholly-otherness in relation to "You shall be holy"

It is not possible to develop in detail all that confronts us on our subject in the Exodus 19 to Leviticus 9 context. However, let us notice how on several counts God's *wholly-otherness* is the basis for understanding how to meet the requirement, "You shall be holy."

During the burning bush encounter with God and on other occasions, Moses experienced not only awe and wonder, but also a strong sense of unworthiness which moved him to surrender to God's will and call. Further, he was desperately determined to have God's *presence* go with him—a dynamic which enabled him to lead Israel out of Egypt. This inner dynamic was a divinely imparted quality of life, there only by God's gracious bestowal. It was in effect an implant of "divine otherness," deriving from the wholly-otherness, or holiness, of God. The linkage or aspect of the nature of man which makes possible this divine implant is the *image of God* that is basic to the humanity of us all.

This implant of a divine quality of life was a *plus* or an added dimension to one's life which was cherished by great pillars of the faith before the time of Christ. It finds a climax in the cleansing, enabling, and abiding presence of the Holy Spirit given at Pentecost, that God intended from the beginning to be normative for His people.

The revelation given at Sinai concerning salvation in its sum of significant aspects (such as altar, priesthood, sacrifices, and sanctuary) have their origin ultimately in God. These all were graciously bestowed to overrule the brokenness and perversity which characterizes the inner life and outward behavior of human beings since the Fall. Thus, when God said to His people, "You shall be holy," the people were able to keep this commandment by accepting, and by faith participating in, His merciful provisions for their salvation or wholeness of life; that is, their holiness. All this is the gracious divine provision for us against the background of the wholly-otherness of God, or of the holiness of God. Thus, meeting the divine requirement, "You shall be holy, for I . . . am holy," is a matter of accepting His gracious provisions.

There is certainly much more to be said on these matters. It will suffice at this point to state that whereas Israel was unique in having entered into covenant with God, and thereby justified apart from any merit or initiative on her part—justification here is a free-caring act on God's part as always. Further, the revelation given concerning altar, priesthood, and sacrifices conveys significant truths about the redemptive plan of God from the foundation of the world (John 17:24; Eph. 1:4; Heb. 4:3). Thus we find that as we follow the Old Testament beginnings of the redemptive plan of God into the New Testament, the various major aspects of this plan have been gloriously fulfilled in the coming of Jesus Christ. The New Testament Gospel writers and others were thoroughly convinced of this and pointed out that Jesus had come to fulfill the Law and the Prophets (e.g., Matt. 5:17; Luke 24:44). All this is related significantly to the *wholly-otherness* of God, enabling us today to meet the requirement laid down many centuries before the time of Jesus.

3. "You shall be holy" in relation to the moral perfection of God

In the Leviticus 19 through Deuteronomy context, we find how God makes clear the way to meet the requirement of being holy over against the background of His holiness or moral perfection. God's people are to live by an ethical code which emphasizes the highest moral values. There is thus the evident concern on God's part that His people establish behavior patterns in conformity with His morally perfect nature. It is in relation to God's moral perfection that we understand how to meet the requirement "You shall be holy, for I . . . am holy."

The guidelines for being holy in everyday living are the Ten Commandments given first in Exod. 20:1-17, repeated in essence here in Leviticus 19, and repeated again as well as expounded upon with ramifications in Deuteronomy. Two points should be made concerning the Ten Commandments. First, the doing of the Ten Commandments in all their varied applications to life was not and is not to be understood as earning merit for one's salvation. Rather the doing of them was to be seen as response to God's will in the context of being already established in a "saved" and "saving" relationship with God. Second, obedience before God in keeping these commandments was and is to be regarded as vital to growth in any covenant or saving relationship with God.

What then is set before us as God's will? It is of special significance that the statement "For I am the Lord your God" is purposely repeated a number of times. This is to reinforce the fact that these laws are not man-made rules but God-given requirements.

Children were to obey and respect their parents, and all shall observe Sabbath days (v. 3). The law concerning children is meant to establish early in life the recognition that life does have its appropriate authorities other than a self-centered authority (a prevailing attitude in our time). Observance of Sabbath days was to be a significant way to acknowledge that God has rightful claim to the totality of one's personal life.

They were not to turn to idols (v. 4). This ran counter to all the religions of the time. The important issue in this is that God alone is to reign in the heart and life of His people as individuals or as a community of believers.

They were to participate as needed in peace offerings (v. 5). The participation in this aspect of worship was to make atonement for sins inadvertently committed and also to help develop a vital relationship between God and His people.

They were to live differently on additional counts; all of which were counter to the way people around them acted. They were to leave gleanings in their grain fields and pickings in their vineyards for the poor. They were never to steal, lie, or deceive, taking care always to be truthful and forthright (v. 11). They were never to give false witness when testifying in court, for this profanes the holy name of God (v. 12); never defraud their neighbors, but rather always be respectful of a neighbor's person and rights (v. 13). They were always to be considerate and helpful concerning the physically handicapped, specifically the deaf and the blind (v. 14), as well as give careful attention to justice in the courts (v. 15). They were commanded never to gossip or slander, but to make every reasonable effort to correct misgiving or misunderstanding with their neighbors (v. 16). They were never to hate or hold any vindictive feelings against anyone (vv. 17-18). Then at the end of verse 18 we read, "You shall love your neighbor as yourself." This turns all of the previous *do nots* or *nevers* into one *do*—a command which Jesus called the *second* great commandment (see Mark 12:31).

It was in giving heed to such stipulations as these that God's people were and are to meet the divine requirement, "You shall be holy," from the standpoint of God's moral perfection, or of living in conformity with His holy nature.

4. "You shall be holy" . . . a word for today

What may we learn from Leviticus 19 about God's instruction concerning holy living in our time? Let us remember the words of Heb. 4:12: "For the word of God is living and active and sharper than any two-edged sword, and piercing as far as the division of soul and spirit, of both joints and marrow, and able to judge the thoughts and intentions of the heart."

The stipulations which God laid down for His people in each instance were contrary to the common practice of the day. We, just as the ancient people of Israel, are "in the world" but are not to be "of the world" (John 17:11, 14). Are we instructed by this point or are we judged? Let the "sword of the Spirit" (Eph. 6:17) do its work.

Being holy, set against the background of God's moral perfection, then, is a matter of seeing to it that one's individual life conforms to the known will of the holy God. Inasmuch as God's will has been spelled out in terms of basic principles for everyday living, it is a matter of carefully applying these principles to all aspects of daily behavior. Jesus in the Sermon on the Mount (Matthew 5—7) does not release us from applying these principles; rather He exhorts us to seek a "higher life" which goes beyond many of these earlier guidelines. Are we instructed by this point or are we judged? Let the "sword of the Spirit" do its work.

It is clear that we are to live by justice, honesty, truthfulness, and helpfulness toward those in need. We are to refrain from gossip and slander. We must harbor no festering grudge and show love toward others. These are aspects of "being holy" in daily life and at the same time tie one to social responsibility. That is, where these aspects of godly living do not prevail in society at large, the responsibility confronting the Christian is to press resourcefully and energetically for correction of such social ills or evils. The prophets in particular make this point clear.

Further, in the early days of Israel's history Moses saw this truth as basic to God's concern as he gave himself completely to the alleviation of the oppression and bondage of the Israelites in Egypt. John Wesley and Phineas F. Bresee of our theological heritage understood this as an all-important aspect of "being holy" more clearly than has been generally perceived today by those under the banner "Called unto Holiness." Are we instructed or are we judged by this point? Let the "sword of the Spirit" do its work.

"Called unto Holiness" is a call to take seriously the command of Lev. 19:2, "You shall be holy, for I the Lord your God am holy." It is a call to accept by faith from the hand of God the gracious provisions for our salvation. In doing this we enter into the newness of a transformed life characterized by the abiding Holy Presence, the blessed Holy Spirit.

"Called unto Holiness" is also a call to establish a manner of living which is in conformity with the holiness or holy nature of God. This is a call to a life which runs counter to much of our modern world. But it is a call to a quality of life and kind of life which the world has always needed.

As the "sword of the Spirit" has instructed us on one aspect of truth or judged us on another, let us live so as to "march" more enthusiastically and aggressively under the banner "Holiness unto the Lord."

9

• **Morris A. Weigelt**

The gate of entire consecration is narrow, but beyond it lies the land of freedom in Christ's love. There the vast boundaries are etched with red—the embroidery of the Cross

The Boundaries of His Love

SCRIPTURE: 2 Cor. 5:12—6:2

TEXT: 2 Cor. 5:14: *For the love of Christ controls us* (RSV).*

I met him in the hospital where we were both patients. He was a troubled young man. His favorite Bible verse was Heb. 6:4: "For it is impossible to restore again to repentance." His second favorite verse was Heb. 10:31: "It is a fearful thing to fall into the hands of the living God." One day in conversation he confided in me: "I like to think of God as my drill sergeant."

Now that young man certainly has an interesting concept of God. There was an element of security in living for a drill ser-

---

*All scripture quotations in this sermon are from the *Revised Standard Version*.

Morris A. Weigelt
Professor of New Testament

84

geant who barks all of the commands and calls all of the turns, but the element of freedom is conspicuously absent. The thesis of this message is: Within the boundaries of the love of Christ there is genuine security and authentic freedom. The life of Christian holiness is a life of security and freedom within the boundaries of the love of Christ.

The whole letter of 2 Corinthians bristles with some of the most difficult pressures Paul had ever known. The stress was incredible. Small wonder that he testifies in chapter 1: "We were so utterly, unbearably crushed." But when the pressures were the most stringent, he reverted to the great truths of the gospel for his strength. I call two of these great truths to your attention.

1. The life of Christian holiness is a life of genuine security within the boundaries of the love of Christ

Paul had been accused, abused, and castigated by the spiritual parasites whom he calls "super-apostles" in the Corinthian setting. In fact, the words of our text today were written before he knew the outcome of the delicate and difficult situation at Corinth. His utter reliance upon God reappears regularly in the letter: "That was to make us rely not on ourselves but on God who raises the dead." "As surely as God is faithful." "Thanks be to God, who in Christ always leads us in triumph." "Our competence is from God." "We have this treasure in earthen vessels,

---

Morris A. Weigelt, in a fascinating confessional manner, shows how "the love of Christ forms the boundaries of my life" (2 Cor. 5:14-15, author's paraphrase). With a strong autobiographical flavor, he reveals the heart of the scripture as an invitation into the "boundaries of the love of Christ"; and he identifies "genuine security and authentic freedom" as the center of Christian holiness. This beautiful sermon is another example of how a preacher can bring the holiness motif to a passage where it is implicit, but not stated.

to show that the transcendent power belongs to God and not to us."

Now in 5:14-15 he declares: "For the love of Christ controls us, because we are convinced that one has died for all; therefore all have died. And he died for all, that those who live might live no longer for themselves but for him who for their sake died and was raised."

"The love of Christ controls us": there lies the secret to genuine security. The word "control" is most interesting. It is the Greek word *sunechō*. Its meanings include: hold together, cohere, sustain, embrace, hold within boundaries, urge on, impel. A translation then might read: "The love of Christ forms the boundaries of my life." A paraphrase might read: "The love of Christ boxes me in."

The boundaries of the love of Christ were forever etched in red at the Cross. Those boundaries form the outlines of genuine security. There is, in fact, no security outside the boundaries of his marvelous love with which He loved us.

The great contest of our lives comes in the moment when we face the choice between our own inadequate securities and His ultimate security. That is precisely the reason why consecration as the entrance to entire sanctification is so difficult for so many. You see, total consecration requires that we dare to release the last inadequate security blanket to find the genuine security in the boundaries of His love.

The final test case is frequently some relatively minor item in our lives, but it symbolizes the control we would prefer to have over our own lives. The test case is as varied as the people who come to that crossroads in life. Ultimately it forces us to face the question: What will be the boundaries of my life? One of my acquaintances came to that crossroads one day nearly 40 years ago now. He knelt at an altar in a little Dakota church. After more than an hour of praying, he shook his head, said, "Nope!", got up, and left to follow a frustrating life. The contest for security. The contest of priorities. The contest of boundaries. These are pivotal points for us all.

Paul could testify to the "super-apostles" and to the whole Corinthian church that the contest no longer raged in his life. The boundaries of the love of Christ emblazoned on history at Calvary were indeed the circumscription of his life. The security was great enough to enable him to face the taunts and the pressures. Security within the boundaries of the love of Christ: That is the life of Christian holiness.

The hymn writer was correct:

> *When darkness seems to hide His face,*
> *I rest on His unchanging grace.*
> *In every high and stormy gale,*
> *My anchor holds within the veil.*

When my body and emotions mutinied against my will and I found myself in the hospital, the storm seemed pretty fierce. I shall not forget the shock that went through my whole being and reverberated for days when the doctor looked me in the eye and declared: "Everyone has his limits and you have certainly violated yours!" I struggled with that for several days.

But I shall also not forget the day when the counselor asked: "What does this whole situation in your life have to say about your faith? Is it a function of faith?"

I thought for a moment and was able to respond: "This situation reflects the violation of limits in physical and emotional areas, but does not reflect any violation of the boundaries of the love of Christ in spiritual terms."

The counselor replied: "Great! Then you will be able to get well quickly!"

There was a marvelous strength in knowing that God's grace provided a genuine security even in the desperation of those days. My own receiving equipment was in weak shape, but underneath were the everlasting arms. The boundaries of the love of Christ still boxed me in. The truths of the gospel had not changed. Praise be to God!

I posit for you today that the life of Christian holiness provides a genuine security within the boundaries of the love of Christ.

2. The life of Christian holiness is a life of authentic freedom within the boundaries of the love of Christ

My friend with the drill-sergeant God had no freedom. He lived a constantly tormented existence. If the security of the boundaries of the love of Christ provided only such intensity of torment, no one would be interested in that kind of religion.

At first glance, our text does not appear to include the element of freedom. Paul willingly submitted to the power and authority of Christ over his life. The freedom element may not be as readily visible. Many people, and I include myself at an early stage in my Christian life, read "control" in this verse to mean a duty-bound existence filled with loyalties and compulsions that drive us to be good, and to be responsible, and to be Christian.

The intensity of our search for freedom is colored by the plague of the sin nature which tempts us to find our own brand of freedom and try to control our own destinies. The control of the sin nature, however, is no freedom at all. Paul colorfully described that tormented existence in Romans 7 as a captivity, an enslavement to the body of death.

Paul understood that the death of Christ had ended the dominion of that ugly monster of the sin nature. He understood that the death of Christ provided a genuine freedom.

He knew that the mental, spiritual, emotional, and physical laws of the universe still stand. He knew that the violation of those laws brought retribution. H. H. Farmer said it well: "When you go against the grain of the universe, you get splinters."

Yes, the only genuine freedom is found by living within those boundaries and cooperating with the laws of the universe rather than bucking them. Paul understood that very well. He had come to the intersection where he had to choose between his own inadequate security and the security which God provides. He chose to live for Christ and Him alone with no reservations and no fine print in the contract—just unreserved commitment. Now he could declare: "He died for all, that those who live might live no longer for themselves but for him who for their sake died and was raised." It was at that point that he entered into the freedom within the boundaries of the love of Christ.

Cooperation with the laws of the spiritual universe brings the only authentic freedom available. I find that process beautifully illustrated in the process of managing a sailboat. When the boat is moving contrary to the wind and the wave, it is a clumsy contraption. It is hardly possible to keep it from capsizing. The sailor must be constantly maneuvering to maintain the balance. The boat is sluggish and contrary—constantly in danger of being upset. But when the little boat is brought into harmony with the wind and the waves, everything changes. The wind fills the sail. The boat gathers speed. The inclination to capsize is past. With beauty and exhilaration it scuds over the surface of the water. It has found its freedom in cooperation with the laws of the wind and the waves.

So it is with things spiritual. Within the boundaries of the love of Christ made visible at the Cross, authentic freedom becomes visible in our lives. The buoyancy of the dynamic of the Holy Spirit changes everything. All of life is now different. Paul speaks in verse 17 of the freedom to be a new creature in Christ. In verse 18 he speaks of the freedom to be a reconciler. In verse 20 he speaks of the freedom to be an ambassador. In verse 1 of chapter 6 he speaks of the freedom to be a fellow worker with God. And in 6:3 ff. he speaks of the freedom to suffer for the Kingdom.

I repeat: The life of Christian holiness is a life of authentic freedom within the boundaries of the love of Christ. "For the love of Christ controls [me]."

This passage, 2 Cor. 5:14-15, has become the bedrock of my faith and life-style. I find in it the essence of the life of Christian holiness. The boundaries of my life are etched with red—the embroidery of the Cross. Within those boundaries I find security even in the days of emotional and physical weariness of a level I have never before encountered. Within those boundaries I find freedom—the freedom to serve and to anticipate the return of Christ (in the words of 1 Thess. 1:9-10).

I do not find "oversell" of the gospel. I do not find healing on demand. I do not find guaranteed prosperity. But I do find strength in the midst of suffering. I find joy in the midst of pain. I find purpose in a world of conflicting claims.

I offer that security and freedom to you in the name of Christ! If you are still struggling with that final contest of total consecration—as I was in my seminary days—you can solve it at these altars. My final contest was created by years of role playing in the church. I played pious and religious with one set of friends and family. I played rebel with others. Soon I could no longer distinguish reality from role playing. I could fool myself so easily. So the narrow gate of total consecration was a contest of coming to the place where my consecration was genuine and not a role—where that giving of myself was authentic and not another smokescreen. It happened in the spring of my senior year. Dr. Earle knelt at my left and several friends at my right. That day I stepped into the boundaries of His love so vividly painted for the whole world at the Cross. I entered and found that the narrow way was the true way of security and freedom.

I invite you to that same narrow gate of entire consecration. I invite you into the boundaries of the love of Christ. I invite you to share the genuine security and authentic freedom available only here!

10

• **Albert L. Truesdale**

It takes more than a "world class"
picnic to bring us to a full knowledge
of Christ as our Sanctifier

To Whom Shall We Go?

SCRIPTURE: John 6

TEXT: *Simon Peter answered him, "Lord, to whom shall we go?*
You have the words of eternal life" (John 6:68, RSV).*

The Gospels record numer-
ous controversies between Jesus and His hearers in which His
followers are clearly "on Jesus' side" in the conflict. The chapter
that precedes our scripture lesson, chapter 5, is a case in point.
That chapter is marked by a sharp conflict between Jesus and
the Jewish religious authorities. In spite of the obvious approval
of God upon His deeds and words, Jesus is completely rejected by
the religious leaders; they never seem to give Him a serious
hearing.

---

*Except as otherwise indicated, all Scripture quotations in this sermon are
from the *Revised Standard Version.*

Albert L. Truesdale
Associate Professor of Philosophy of Religion
and Christian Ethics

One graphic incident in chapter 5 illustrates their rejection of Jesus: His healing of the paralytic at the Pool of Bethesda. After a 38-year illness, the man was restored to health by Jesus, but not without raising the rancor of the Pharisees. Wholly unable to appreciate the magnificence of what had occurred, blind to the worth of persons because of their distorted understanding of the law, the Pharisees could see only that Jesus had committed the "scandalous act" of working on the Sabbath (5:16). Although Jesus' answer to His troublers, "My Father is working still, and I am working" (5:17), allows no refutation, the Pharisees' rejection of Jesus went untempered. Their opposition to Him moved ponderously towards the Cross.

In our chapter, the conflict between Jesus and His hearers continues. But here the controversy takes an alarming turn. No longer is the conflict between Jesus and those who have rejected Him outright, but between Jesus and many of those who have followed Him, who have received His words, rejoiced in the miracles, and exulted in His proclamation of the gospel.

In this conflict you and I, as Christ's disciples, are directly involved. Whereas in chapter 5 the Jews had ignited or provoked the conflict, in chapter 6 Jesus is the One who demands specific, decisive responses from His followers. In chapter 5 Jesus' disciples were there as observers, each of us perhaps feeling as though we are the most conspicuous one in the large crowd.

John 6 is the context from which Albert L. Truesdale reflects Jesus' demanding appeal. His use of collateral material supporting his principal burdens skillfully tells a "story" with theological affirmations which, while not stated, are necessarily present. He closes with the "magnificent resolution" through complete submission, making sanctification a condition of "eternal life" (Rom. 6:22). "To whom have I gone?" graphically portrays the conclusion of the matter, showing that, after all, the holiness message is found ultimately in Jesus Christ.

Now I cannot evade His questions, cannot cheer Jesus on as He interrogates my neighbor, cannot say to the Pharisees, "He is right, and you had better listen to Him!" Try, maybe, but His eyes are fixed on me.

1. A crisis of discipleship

The contents of our scripture lesson constitute one of the major crises in Jesus' ministry. Its contrasts are breathtaking. When it opens, the multitudes seek Jesus; when it closes, He is almost deserted, attended only by the Twelve, one of whose allegiance is suspect. In the beginning the multitudes are "fed"; when it closes, only the Twelve want the "bread" Jesus has to offer. When the curtain rises on this drama, the multitudes are ready to make Jesus king; when they go down on the last act, He is the one "despised and rejected by men; a man of sorrows, and acquainted with grief" (Isa. 53:3).

At first, He is viewed as the long-expected prophet; at the end of the chapter these same admirers dismiss Him as a maker of irrational statements and demands. At the chapter's commencement, Jesus is at the peak of popular acclaim; by the time it concludes, our Lord is at a low point of rejection. It begins with an acclamation by the many and closes with an affirmation by the few. It opens with hunger of one kind and closes with the hunger of another. In it are two different hopes and two different disappointments.

What could have happened in between these two points to produce such contrasts? What went wrong? The answer introduces important questions to which each disciple of Christ must respond. The conflict at hand is over what it will mean for a follower of Jesus to confess Him Lord of all.

After having used the lad's barley loaves and two fish to feed the weary multitude, Jesus and His disciples at night made their way by boat across the Sea of Galilee to Capernaum (6:15-21).

But on the next day the people—we are not told how many—came by ship to Capernaum seeking Jesus (22-24).

Now, we might expect that such diligence would be rewarded by Jesus with warm greetings to the travelers. Maybe there would be "a little fish and bread upon the fire," maybe some light talk about the weather, or "the poor construction of boats these days." At any rate, surely the toil of the trip would now disappear in the warm glow of laudatory words from Jesus.

But not so. None of this. Not one "Hello," "Good morning," "Nice to see you," or "I can't tell you how happy I am to see you."

Instead, rebuke! And here the crisis erupts. Gone now are the pastoral scenes of yesterday, the colorful setting of that "world class" picnic, and the miracles which Jesus performed on "those who were diseased" (v. 2).

Now the air is tense; piercing words are spoken by Jesus that accuse His hearers—words that call for a significantly different estimate of Him: "Truly, truly, I say to you, you seek me, not because you saw signs, but because you ate your fill of the loaves" (v. 26).

Simply put, Jesus forces this conflict because these followers have been *seeking Him for the wrong reasons*. They have sought him not principally because of *who He is*, but because of what they *could use Him for*—for what *they could get out of Him*. To them He was chiefly a utility, a heavenly caterer. They followed Him for loaves and fishes. He must do their bidding.

They wanted Him to be the long-expected Messiah, no doubt about this, but only so long as they could retain "definition rights." *They* would be the ones to decide what it would mean for Him to be "the Christ."

Now it becomes a question of who is following whom. The entire crisis comes down to this: Who will decide what it means for Jesus to be the Christ—Jesus or His followers? As Jesus' words make clear, the outcome is not all in doubt. Jesus refused to be their utility. What is in doubt is whether these followers will renounce their claim to self-sovereignty and their cherished desire to follow Jesus on their own terms. Will they surrender their desires to manipulate the Christ—to place Him at their own bidding? Will they embrace Him as Lord of all and allow Him who is the Bread of Life to become the ordering center of their lives?

The problem with these followers was that who He *is* did not radically define who they *were.*

2. A crisis that demands a response

Jesus confronts His followers with the question: "Which bread will be your chief pursuit—the bread that perishes, or the bread that is eternal life?" Clearly, a crisis in the relationship between Jesus and His followers has been reached. They cannot advance in their walk with Him unless, on His own terms, He is invited to reign at the center of their lives and from this new center to reorder and reconstitute the entire range of life.

It is highly instructive that the miraculous feeding of the 5,000, the distribution of the loaves and fishes, did not in any way guarantee that they would fully embrace Christ as Lord. No number of miracles, only abandonment of ourselves to His will can lead to a complete knowledge of what it means to call Jesus "the Bread of Life," *our* Life, *our* Sanctifier.

So far in the chapter the people are sure that "loaves and fishes" are their greatest need. But their estimates are completely wrong. So long as these are their prevailing interests, they will not know Christ *as He is*. Instead, they will continue to reduce Him to their own dimensions. Clearly, they need a major change in the way they think about Him, and this will lead to an equally major change in the way they understand themselves. Earlier, Jesus had admonished the smaller circle of disciples, "Seek ye first the kingdom of God, and his righteousness" (Matt. 6:33, KJV). Now He tells his followers that their most urgent and comprehensive need is not for the "food which perishes, but for the food which endures to eternal life, which the Son of man will give to you" (v. 27).

The "bread that perishes" represents far more than what is baked in an oven. It symbolizes all our physical, economic, social, and emotional needs and desires. If these interests claim our chief allegiance and energies, Jesus says, they make impossible the victorious discipleship, wholeness, peace, and hope for which we long. A discipleship that is divided between allegiance to Christ on the one hand, and a lingering unwillingness to commit every phase of life to Him on the other, cannot achieve the complete joy of Christ's reign as Lord over us. Such "discipleship" will always be plagued by conflicts and frustration.

Simply put, throughout the midsection of this chapter Jesus invites His followers to abandon all efforts to dictate the terms of discipleship. He calls us to relinquish all lingering attempts to mix self-sovereignty with professed love for Him. The two are hopelessly incompatible. Either Jesus will be Lord of all, or He will not be Lord at all.

These followers continue to demand signs. They insist on putting Jesus to the test (v. 30). "Give us more bread," they say, "and then we will believe!" They are wrong. Their demands come from reluctant, divided hearts which no number of "signs" could overcome. So long as this condition holds, the demands for "bread" will continue. What is needed is an abrupt end to all attempts to bargain with Christ about the shape and range of His Lordship.

Now it is clear why Jesus tells His followers bluntly, "I am the bread of life; he who comes to me shall not hunger, and he who believes in me shall never thirst" (v. 35). "Come to me"—these are the key words; "come" not to the sensational aspects of signs, but away from the old self-centeredness, the old struggle against the complete will of God, and to Him as the Lord who possesses and completely reorients the whole person. Come to Him who cleanses and sanctifies all of life.

These questions must be faced by every disciple. Who will define discipleship? Who will decide the dimensions of Christ's Lordship? There is only one sufficient answer: "I am the living bread which came down from heaven; if any one eats of this bread, he will live for ever; and the bread which I shall give for the life of the world is my flesh" (v. 51).

At this point in the chapter the atmosphere is charged with anticipation. The issues and risks are clear. Decisions must be made. Futures wait to be molded.

3. Two types of decisions

John observes, "After this many of his disciples drew back and no longer went about with him" (v. 66). "No," they said, "a Christ who asks this much, who wants to be the Lord of my whole life, is simply asking too much!" "If you can't accept us on our own terms," the crowd said, "then good-bye! We will find another Messiah. It's a buyer's market anyway."

And off they went, away from the Bread of Life.

Now silence follows. And silence is followed by one of the most penetrating questions in the New Testament. Almost deserted now, Jesus turns to the Twelve and asks, "Do you also wish to go away?" (v. 67). What Jesus asked of them, He also asks of you and me, "Will you also leave Me?"

Now comes a response so filled with faith and affirmation that it spills over as exultation and invites us to do the same. Peter, speaking for the group, says, "Lord, to whom shall we go? You have the words of eternal life; and we have believed, and have come to know, that you are the Holy One of God" (vv. 68-69).

Ah, this is the response for which we have been searching. In this response there is no more competition between Jesus and His disciples, no bickering about the cost of the Kingdom, no bargaining about what Lordship means or testing Jesus from the "safety" of one's own self-centeredness.

"Lord, to whom shall we go? You have the words of eternal

life." The words spoken by Peter open the door for sanctification of the entire person by Christ who *is* eternal life. When believers completely abandon all attempts to limit how He can be the Bread of Life, then He can dispense himself as the Bread of Life into every part of our lives. Then will we know the full meaning of His promise, "I came that [you] may have life, and have it abundantly" (John 10:10).

What a magnificent resolution of the crisis!—complete consecration to Christ who is "our wisdom, our righteousness and sanctification and redemption" (1 Cor. 1:30). This is what Jesus also desired from those followers who left Him. This is His call to every Christian.

Sanctification means joyfully affirming throughout the full range of our spirit, "You have the words of eternal life. I come to You without reservation!" The fruit of complete submission to Christ as Lord of all, Paul says, is sanctification, and its end is eternal life (Rom. 6:22).

4. To whom have I gone?

To the crisis so graphically portrayed in this chapter there are two possible responses. One leads away from Christ, the other leads more deeply into Him. One leads at best to an ambiguous, tenuous relationship with Christ, at base always inclining away from Him. The other response ends in a joyous, extravagant submission of one's entire being to Him. One response retains the self as sovereign, the other enthrones the Christ as Lord of all.

The question: On which side of the conflict do I stand? By which response am I characterized? To whom have I gone? To whom shall you go? Will it be to some self-conceived "messiah" who will tolerate divided allegiance, or to the Christ who alone has the words of life?

11

● **Terrell C. Sanders, Jr.**

For the Christian race we prepare, persevere, and look to Christ

Our Supreme Example

TEXT: *Therefore, since we are surrounded by such a great cloud of witnesses, let us throw off everything that hinders and the sin that so easily entangles, and let us run with perseverance the race marked out for us. Let us fix our eyes on Jesus, the author and perfecter of our faith, who for the joy set before him endured the cross, scorning its shame, and sat down at the right hand of the throne of God. Consider him who endured such opposition from sinful men, so that you will not grow weary and lose heart* (Heb. 12:1-3, NIV).

As you read this text, you can almost hear the roar of the great crowd in the amphitheater as the runners line up for a race. The excitement rises and the tension builds as the start of the race draws near. The spectators cheer as the participants sprint forward from the starting blocks.

Terrell C. Sanders, Jr.
President

The writer to the Hebrew Christians indicates that the Christians are the runners, and the spectators may be the great host of witnesses mentioned in the roll call of the faithful in the preceding chapter.

The runners are encouraged by the growing crowd of spectators who surround the racetrack in the arena. On the other hand, it may be that the Christian participants are encouraged by the knowledge that so many have successfully completed the same race that they are presently engaged in. The truth probably lies in both of these concepts.

Be this as it may, there is a large crowd of people witnessing this race in which we are engaged. There is a host of people in our churches and homes who are observing our progress. There is also a large crowd in the wider community of our world who by observing our efforts are encouraged or discouraged concerning receiving Christ as Savior. The manner in which we run the race of the Christian life has a tremendous influence on them.

My deep desire and prayer for you is that you may successfully run and complete the race which is "marked out" for you.

1. In order to accomplish this, there must be proper preparation for the race

Our scripture says, "Let us throw off everything that hinders and the sin that so easily entangles" (v. 1, NIV).

To be properly prepared, there must be personal discipline and disentanglement from all that will hinder us in the race. The runners in Roman races stripped themselves of all extra clothing and trained to rid themselves of all extra body weight in order to

---

President Terrell C. Sanders' sermon taken from Heb. 12:1-3 is textual, again the simplest form of exposition. Its power is in its simplicity and description. He very properly closes with an appeal from verse 2, "Let us fix our eyes on Jesus."

run the race successfully. In our day, people who are serious about competitive running spend many hours in special exercises, diet control, and in 50 or 60 miles of running each week.

In like manner the Christian must discipline himself and lay aside anything and everything which will hinder his progress in the race. Life has a way of getting cluttered with excess baggage until one gets so burdened that he can no longer run the race effectively. William Barclay calls attention to this truth when he writes: "There is in life an essential duty in discarding things. There may be habits, there may be pleasures, there may be self-indulgences, there may be associations which hold us back and down. They have to be shed as an athlete sheds his outer cloak as he goes to the starting mark. Whatever holds us back must go" ("Hebrews," *The Daily Study Bible,* p. 196).

The New Testament writer did not specify what it is that we must lay aside. He does make it clear that whatever hinders our spiritual progress must be discarded. It may be ever so legitimate, and others may possess it. However, if it hinders your progress, you must shed it like a runner laying aside his warmup suit.

Proper preparation for this race also involves personal purity. We must not only lay aside "every weight" but also "the sin that so easily entangles" us.

"The sin" in this verse does not mean some particular sin known as a "besetting" sin, but the carnal nature itself. In explaining this verse, H. Orton Wiley wrote: "The word for 'sin' as used here is *hamartian* 'sin' in the singular, not sins in the plural. The word has reference to 'sin' itself, the heart condition from which all sin flows" (*The Epistle to the Hebrews,* p. 385).

W. T. Purkiser substantiates this interpretation: "Above all, the Christian must be rid of 'the sin which doth so easily beset him.' This is not one particular sin. It is the sin, a generic term— the very principle of sin itself" (*Beacon Bible Expositions,* 11:103).

The carnal nature is like a flowing garment which wraps itself around us, clinging so closely to us that it impedes our progress and tends to trip us, causing us to fall and lose the race. This sin must be done away with if we hope to complete the race.

Dr. Wiley makes this clear in the following statement: "This sin manifests itself according to our temperament, condition or circumstances; but it is *the sin* itself that we are commanded to put away promptly—do it and be done with it" (*Hebrews,* p. 386).

Thank God! There is a remedy for all sin, which not only involves forgiveness of our sins, but the experience of heart cleansing through the baptism with the Holy Spirit.

The apostle Peter understood this when he said of Cornelius and his household: "God, who knows the heart, showed that he accepted them by giving the Holy Spirit to them, just as he did to us. He made no distinction between us and them, for he purified their hearts by faith" (Acts 15:8-9, NIV).

2. To run this race successfully, we must persevere to the finish

"Let us run with perseverance the race marked out for us" (Heb. 12:1, NIV). The race of life is not a quick, 100-yard dash, but a long-distance run requiring tremendous endurance. To persevere in the New Testament sense is not a passive endurance, but an aggressive, active perseverance in pursuit of a great goal.

In the life of the Christian and the minister, there is no place to quit, no place to drop out. We must run and keep on running until we reach our goal. The long-distance runner learns to pace himself for the long run. He has learned to control his speed, his breathing, and make adjustments for the weather and terrain in order to persevere until the end of the race. He will not entertain the thought of dropping out of the race. He will not quit the race until he crosses the finish line.

3. In order to be successful in this great race, our perception must be of Jesus only

"Let us fix our eyes on Jesus" (v. 2, NIV). He is both our Goal and our supreme Example in the race which is "marked out" for us as Christians. The Christian runner is literally to "look away to Jesus." He may glance at the crowd of witnesses; but above all, he must keep his eyes fixed on Jesus. He cannot spend time admiring the scenery, he cannot look at the spectators, he must not let other runners distract him. He must keep his eyes fixed on Jesus!

The story is told of the "Miracle Mile" in which two famous runners, known at that time as the fastest men on earth, were racing in Vancouver in 1954. One had led the race all the way; but near the finish line, he looked over his shoulder to see where his competitor was. In that instant his competitor passed him and won the race.

In this great race there is no time to look back, no time to look to others, no time to look at self—our eyes must be fixed on Jesus.

Dr. G. B. Williamson wrote: "One absolute essential is to keep a fixed gaze upon Jesus, the author and finisher of our faith. Look to anyone else and eventually be disillusioned and disappointed, look at yourself and succumb to despair" (*Holiness for Every Day,* p. 116).

The devil has many tricks to get us to look at someone or something other than Jesus. However, our safety and guarantee of success is to keep our gaze fixed on Jesus, our Supreme Example and Source of inspiration. He is the One who has blazed the trail and pioneered the way into the presence of the Heavenly Father for us. In being the "author" or Pioneer of our salvation, He did "taste death for every man" (Heb. 2:9) and entered the presence of the Father and "sat down at the right hand" of God (1:3, NIV).

Because He successfully ran the race before us and pioneered a way into the presence of the Father, we too may join Him in triumph in our heavenly home with the Father.

The joy of the race of the Christian life is to enjoy His fellowship as we travel this journey, and to know that we shall share in His victory throughout eternity.

Conclusion: In most races, there is but one winner. However, in the Christian race all may win. Those who run the marathon races often say, "To complete the race is to win." This is especially true of the Christian race. Jesus said, "He who stands firm to the end will be saved" (Matt. 10:22, NIV).

Our Lord Jesus Christ "endured the cross, scorning its shame, and sat down at the right hand of the throne of God" (Heb. 12:2, NIV). We too will have some difficult places in the race of life, but as the songwriter has put it, "It will be worth it all when we see Jesus."

12

• **Ralph Earle**

*Self-crucifixion must replace self-coronation
or the fruit of the Spirit will remain something
dreamed of but not experienced*

Crucified with Christ

SCRIPTURE: Gal. 2:20; 3:1-3; 5:16-25

TEXT: *I have been crucified with Christ and I no longer live, but
Christ lives in me. The life I live in the body, I live by faith
in the Son of God, who loved me and gave himself for me
(Gal. 2:20, NIV).* The fruit of the Spirit is love, joy, peace,
patience, kindness, goodness, faithfulness, gentleness and
self-control (Gal. 5:22-23).*

Every resurrection must be
preceded by a crucifixion. You can't come to Easter Sunday
without going through Good Friday. That's a chronological fact,
but it has theological implications. You can't reach the empty
tomb unless you take the road that goes through the Garden of

---

*Unless otherwise indicated, all Scripture quotations in this sermon are from
the *New International Version.*

Ralph Earle
Distinguished Professor Emeritus of New Testament

Gethsemane and past the cross of Calvary. One of the great paradoxes of Christianity is simply this: You have to die to live!

George Mueller, that great man of faith in Bristol, England, said: "There was a day when I died, utterly died." And on his 90th birthday he wrote these words: "I was converted in November, 1825, but I only came into the full surrender of the heart four years later, in July, 1829. The love of money was gone; the love of place was gone; God, God alone, became my portion." George Mueller also said: "After I was filled with the Spirit, I learned more about the Scriptures in four hours than I had learned in the previous four years."

Vincent Taylor, a great British New Testament scholar of our generation, made this statement: "Sin is self-coronation." I should like to put alongside of that this suggestion: "Sanctification is self-crucifixion." Ultimately we either let self be crucified with Christ, and Christ crowned as Lord of all in our lives, or we crown self as lord of all, and leave Christ hanging on the Cross as far as we are concerned.

Jesus said, "If anyone would come after me, he must deny himself and take up his cross [that's self-crucifixion] and follow me." Then He went on to say: "Whoever loses his life for me will find it" (Matt. 16:24-25). We sing, "Let me lose myself and find it, Lord, in Thee." This underscores a profound truth. You cannot really find your true self, your "Christed" self, unless and until you lose your false self, your carnal self, through full commitment to Christ.

Ralph Earle is the Distinguished Professor Emeritus of New Testament. Taking two passages from Galatians, he emphasizes the crucifixion of the carnal mind as a precondition of the fruit of the Spirit. His illustrations are pertinent to his burdens, and he makes his evangelistic appeal on the ground of the final illustration; that is, "Are you willing to let the Holy Spirit enable you to make your consecration complete?"

1. The crucifixion of the carnal self

There is no more striking application of the truth we have been considering than that found in our text, Gal. 2:20. In the King James Version the first part reads: "I am crucified with Christ: nevertheless I live; yet not I, but Christ liveth in me." But the Greek does not say "nevertheless"; it says *ouketi,* "no longer." Actually, the first clause of the verse declares, "I have been crucified with Christ" (perfect tense in Greek). The second clause reads: "and I no longer live." The "I" is expressed with emphasis in the Greek by *egō,* which we have taken over into English as *ego.* In other words, what Paul is saying is this: "Christ has taken the place of the carnal ego in control of my life."

We say that in order to be justified—or, as we popularly call it, "converted"—we have to repent and believe; and in order to be sanctified wholly, we have to consecrate and believe. But consecration has its climax in the full and final surrender of our will to God's will. Self-submission always precedes self-crucifixion. God cannot sanctify the unsurrendered will.

2. The work of faith

In Gal. 3:3 Paul writes: "Are you so foolish? After beginning with the Spirit, are you now trying to attain your goal by human effort?" The Greek verb for "attain your goal" is *epiteleō.* It is compounded of *epi,* "upon," and *telos,* "end." So it suggests "reach that end." It may be translated "made perfect" (KJV) or "being perfected" (NASB).

We cannot sanctify ourselves by our own efforts. Sanctification is the work of the Holy Spirit in the human heart. Some people say: "Jesus is my Savior; the Holy Spirit is my Sanctifier." This is hardly a valid distinction. The correct testimony is this: "I was regenerated by the Holy Spirit through faith in Jesus Christ; I was also sanctified by the Holy Spirit through faith in Jesus Christ." In both cases the Holy Spirit is the active Agent, and He works in answer to our faith in Christ's finished work for us on the Cross.

What is this faith that makes possible our sanctification? Too many people interpret the word "believe" as mainly intellectual. But it must also be volitional if it is going to effect the results we want.

John G. Paton was a missionary to the New Hebrides. Immediately upon his arrival he was confronted with the seemingly insoluble problem that still faces Bible translators around the world: the fact that most languages of primitive tribes have few if any abstract terms. They have concrete terms for tree, rock, house, etc., but nothing remotely resembling peace, joy, or love, to say nothing of grace. Particularly, how are you going to tell people to believe in Jesus where there is no such concept as "believe" in their language?

One day Paton was sitting in his crude hut, trying to translate the New Testament. He was utterly frustrated at the lack of any word in the native language that would convey the idea of "believe."

Just then an old man walked in. Weary from a long walk, he slumped down in a chair. As he did so, he said in the native dialect, "I'm leaning my whole weight on this chair."

Immediately something clicked inside Paton's brain. Quickly he asked the man to repeat what he had just said. And in the New Testament for that tribe "believe on" became "lean your whole weight on." That is exactly what faith is. When we lean our whole weight on Jesus, we find that He will never let us down. And when we trust Him implicitly and completely to sanctify us through and through (1 Thess. 5:23), we can rest in the sweet assurance that the Holy Spirit has cleansed our hearts from all sin and filled them with His sanctifying presence. It is God's gracious gift to us, through faith.

3. The fruit of the Spirit

One of the great contrasts in the Bible is that between "the works of the flesh" (5:19-21, KJV) and "the fruit of the Spirit" (vv. 22-23). One almost hears the hiss of the old serpent, Satan, in "the works of the flesh." Every one of them is divisive: "sexual immorality, impurity and debauchery; idolatry and witchcraft; hatred, discord, jealousy, fits of rage, selfish ambition, dissensions, factions and envy; drunkenness, orgies, and the like." Such a sordid list!

What a tremendous contrast when we move on to verse 22! "*But*"——underline that word twice——"the fruit of the Spirit is love, joy, peace, patience, kindness, goodness, faithfulness, gentleness and self-control."

We often hear people talk about "the fruits of the Spirit." But this is clearly unscriptural. "Fruit" is singular; and every one of the characteristics of that fruit mentioned here is unifying.

The first is "love." The Greek word is *agapē*. It means "unselfish love," which seeks the best good of the one we love. It is a love that involves the whole person—emotions, intellect, and will. It is the same word which is used in the great "Love Chapter," 1 Corinthians 13.

Why are "fruit" and "is" singular? John Wesley gave the best answer to that question. In his *Explanatory Notes Upon the New Testament* he says of "love" here: "It is the root of all the rest." That is, the fruit of the Spirit *is* love, which expresses itself in "joy, peace, patience, kindness," etc. In Greek grammar we would say that the other eight terms are epexegetical of "love"——they exegete its meaning and applications.

This observation by John Wesley is entirely logical. The Holy Spirit is God; and "God is love" (1 John 4:8, 16). So when we are filled with the Spirit, we are filled with love. This love will then manifest itself in the ways enumerated here.

Love first manifests itself in *joy.* What is joy? Someone has said: "Joy is the echo of God's life within us," and "Joy is the reflection of spiritual health in the soul." This reminds us of what we read in the Old Testament: "The joy of the Lord is your strength" (Neh. 8:10). A joyless Christian is a weak Christian, and he or she can't help others. Years ago I heard a man say: "A religion that makes a man look sick will never cure the ills of this world." How true! We should show this joy on our faces.

The next expression of love is *peace*. The Greek word is *eirēnē*, from which we get the girl's name Irene. Every Irene should be a peaceful person!

When we are justified freely, "we have peace with God through our Lord Jesus Christ" (Rom. 5:1). When we are sanctified wholly, we have "the peace of God, which transcends all understanding" (Phil. 4:7). The songwriter called it "the peace that comes by giving all." And that is the price we have to pay for the deepest peace of soul.

Dr. J. B. Chapman used to say that peace is the consciousness of adequate resources to meet all the emergencies of life. When our hearts are filled with the Holy Spirit, we know that we have that adequate resource.

The third characteristic of love is *patience*. As long as we associate with other people, we have to be patient and long-suffering because we differ in personality. Even the most devoted husband and wife will find some such personality differences that call for patience if life is to move smoothly. Different backgrounds, different eating habits, different likes and dislikes, different times for rising and going to bed—all these, and many others, require patience with each other. Otherwise there will not be peace in the home, and finally no peace in our hearts.

The fourth characteristic is *kindness.* In 1 Cor. 13:4 we find these last two put together: "Love is patient, love is kind." Instinctively we feel that one of the main manifestations of love is kindness. But it takes patience, many times, to be kind. They go together.

The fifth characteristic of love is *goodness.* Too often this

110

term is misunderstood. Someone says: "I don't lie, cheat, steal, or do anything wrong; I'm good!" But that doesn't make a person good.

The best definition of goodness I have ever read is that by Charles R. Erdman in his commentary. He says that goodness is "love in action." That hits the nail right on the head. I am not good because of anything I *don't* do; I am only good as I act in love.

This should be a constant challenge to all of us. Do I always act in love? Do you? Let's ask God to help us by His indwelling Spirit to act always in the spirit of love. This is a part of our growth in grace.

The next characteristic is *faithfulness*. The King James Version says "faith." The Greek word is *pistis*, which means both "faith" and "faithfulness." But here the context clearly indicates that it is "faithfulness" that Paul is talking about. The Holy Spirit will help us to be faithful to our responsibilities.

The next manifestation is *gentleness*. The main symbol of the Holy Spirit is the dove, as shown at Jesus' baptism. The dove is a very gentle creature, noted for its soft, cooing sound.

In what is commonly known as the Song of Solomon we find the expression, "Thou hast doves' eyes" (1:15, KJV). But we know some professing Christians who have hawks' eyes. They can see the least little fault and magnify it into a big thing. Probably most of us have seen a hawk, high in the sky, suddenly take a power dive, grab a tiny chicken or field mouse, and carry it away to devour it. How can the hawk see a small object from such a distance? Because it has telescopic sight.

If we glory in the fact that we have "spiritual discernment" to spot people's little faults, we ought to ask God to remove our telescopic lens and replace it with a wide-angle lens. Then we can see things in their proper perspective, understand somewhat of people's backgrounds, and treat them with loving compassion instead of cold criticism. The Holy Spirit will help us to do this.

The last characteristic is *self-control*. This can often be the deciding factor between success and failure in our Christian life. The Holy Spirit can help us with this too.

Rees Howells was saved during the famous Welsh revival. As is still true with newly converted Irish and Welsh young men, he immediately began to preach and win souls to Christ. But one day the Holy Spirit began to deal with him about his need of making a full commitment to Christ and of his being filled with the Spirit. He tells how he spent five days dying out to his own will and desires.

Finally he felt that the Lord said to him, "You must get this thing decided by six o'clock this evening." He prayed more earnestly, trying to surrender his will full to God's will. The afternoon dragged by and six o'clock approached. Desperately Howells begged for more time. But God said, "No."

Finally it was only a few minutes before six, and he was almost in a panic. The Lord said, "Are you willing to let Me have My way fully in your life?" In desperation, Howells cried, "Lord, I want to be willing to surrender my will completely to Your will, but I can't seem to do it." Then the Holy Spirit whispered in his soul, "Are you willing to be made willing?" Howells gasped out, "Yes," and immediately full peace came to his heart. Are you willing to let the Holy Spirit enable you to make your consecration complete?